REBUILT
— Beginning the Ending —
RENEW | RESTORE | REBUILD

My world was completely shattered.
Until God began building me back together.
He is taking every shattered piece.
And He is using it for His glory.
For He knew I needed to be broken.
AGAIN!
So this time the rebuilding would include just Him.
God is over everything.
God is my source.

God is in the midst of her
She shall not be moved.
God shall help her
Just at the break of dawn
Psalm 46:5
~Christina Cruz-Mendez

REBUILT
Beginning the Ending

Copyright © 2020
ISBN: 978-1-9161791-4-1

Published by:
Gracehouse Publishing
56, Gosport Road, Walthamstow,
London, United Kingdom, E17 7LY

Unless otherwise indicated, all Scripture quotations are taken from the New King James Version (NKJV) of the Bible.

All rights reserved.
No portion of this book may be used without the written permission of the publisher, with the exception of brief excerpts in magazines, articles, reviews, etc.

Contents

Dedication	05
Acknowledgments	07
Introduction: Beginning the Ending	13
PIECE 1 You Survived	17
PIECE 2 I'm Backwards	27
PIECE 3 My Perfect Storm	35
PIECE 4 Reboot – System Processing	41
PIECE 5 How Long	53
PIECE 6 What Cave Are You In	61
PIECE 7 Destroy It	79
PIECE 8 When Beauty Is Toxic	87
PIECE 9 No More Relapse	97
PIECE 10 Where Is Your Support System	109
PIECE 11 Love Never Fails	123
PIECE 12 I Need A Cover	135
PIECE 13 Hope For A Tree (Like Me)	149
PIECE 14 Beauty Inside	155
PIECE 15 Matters Of The Heart	165

PIECE 16 Make Frequent Stops And Rest	177
PIECE 17 Attitude Is Everything	183
PIECE 18 Powerful Prayers	189
PIECE 19 Push Past Pain	197
PIECE 20 Seasons Of Change	205
PIECE 21 Under Construction	211
PIECE 22 All Grown Up	221
PIECE 23 The Broken One	229
PIECE 24 In God's Collage	241
PIECE 25 Reminders Along The Way	251
PIECE 26 Let It Be	257
PIECE 27 More Than A Thorn	265
PIECE 28 Black Butterflies	273
PIECE 29 The Victor	283
PIECE 30 Pulling Through The Promise	293
Appendix	303

For Cassandra Isabella
My Baby Girl, always.

REBUILT: Beginning the Ending

Acknowledgments

I must begin by acknowledging the first One that inspired me to write in the first place and to the One that saved me from a life that needed saving. This makes me forever grateful and thankful to God My Father. At the age of 39 I had a heart to heart conversation with God on the weekend of February 6, 2015. That was the weekend that I rededicated my life back to God during a retreat at which I was supposed to be speaking at. This time, I had to decline the slot to minister 3 weeks prior to leaving and allow God to minister to my life that was in desperate need of saving.

My immediate family you are my world, nothing else comes close to what you all have done for me. Juan Antonio – what a man of valor! Thank you for supporting me, receiving me and always helping to propel me into becoming a stronger woman of God. This definitely isn't a fairytale! This isn't puppy love, addictive love, euphoric love, or butterfly tummy love! This is COVENANT love that says, I am with you always as you are with me. It is where the two become one. This is a tale on a lifetime of faith and forgiveness. So many cute poetic stories there are, yet ours is a walk and work in progress for life! It's the good, the bad and the ugliest ugly you would ever see! PERFECT right... Because that is where and how God sealed this with the blood covenant right before Him. On this pair, He placed His perfection on our imperfections. We walk by faith and not by sight, all goes beyond a pretty picture. That we call an agape practice of love, that's unconditional my friend, my partner, my half... I love who we are-it is very unique.

Cassandra Isabella —you are my gem. Your prayers and steadfast love impacted our world. Sammy Isaiah —you are my "Hammville," my button of joy! My little gentleman.

Mobbie, you are amazing! I testify here of our upbringing but through it all you fought to bring us further and encourage your kids. You set a beautiful example for us. You instilled in us to do more. I LOVE YOU and I am thankful to be attached to your hip still.

Acknowledgments

Creatan, big bro, you know I love you and that I am so proud of you. Keep representing Coastie!

Cris, you are my covenant sister and true example of sisterhood. Anthony —yes, I am probably the only one that still calls you that so… ANT! You are such a pillar! Together you and Cris have helped me discover SO MUCH in Christ! I will never forget any word you have spoken over me because nothing ever fell to the ground. I rely on our covenant relationship and know that we are forever knit together.

MJ, what can I say but that I could never have found a friend like you! You are God-sent! I will never forget the words that you shared with me each time that I called with a tear stained face. I tried to release all of that pain. I wanted everything to be over and for me to be better. You said to me clearly, "This isn't going to happen overnight Christina! Rome wasn't built in a day and neither are you. It takes time."

Every day, yes I know. I am being built back up.

Jenny, you encouraged me to keep writing and quickly. I know that you were diligent to remind me and help me believe that these words were with a mandate. "YOU'RE AN INSPIRATION," you told me. I would have to agree that so are you.

My MUI Sisters in Christ that helped encourage me over these days, months and years. There is no better way but the route of truth based on a godly sisterhood. The ones that labor with me, cry with me and war with me. Thank you all so much!

Rose, you know that I am so glad we have reconnected! We grew up, now we are closer. Nothing but shared LOVE!

My dear counselor and friend Noel Clark, you took the time to encourage me regularly to work on myself and find my source of strength in the Highest power which is God. Your words and time spent listening to my redundancy will never go unseen. You have been a huge place of validation. When you asked, "Who will validate you?" You were one of them!

Larry, my friend and editor! You supported me in everything! Words alone aren't enough to express the gratitude.

To the ministers of the gospel and my spiritual mothers that would speak words of encouragement, hope and direction over my life. I will never forget the Word of the Lord that came forth in the most desolate times of my life, duly noted as "cleaning house!" It just took me some time to realize that the "cleaning house" was meant for me specifically and not just what was happening in my sphere. There was something in my house {temple} that was trying to destroy my purpose. I knew exactly what that was. I just wanted to be the only hoarder and self-deceiver.

> ***"There is a way that appears to be right, but in the end it leads to death."*** Proverbs 14:12 (New International Version)

I can't let that happen anymore…not at all. God help me!

Let's go through this restoration process already. I have to accept that I am officially checked in to God's Rehabilitation Center for LIFE! It is called my process of survival! This was my eye-opening "kick start" and in the Name of the Lord will be one for others. This was beginning the ending of my own personal madness.

I can only pray that the people reading this will find a place throughout these pages where they can relate, where they can be honest and open up. I pray that they take the words put together in these pages and find their own renewal that could be vital to their situation NOW. I pray that they experience a lasting restoration and that they will allow the Lord to REBUILD all that He has destined for. As I unfold my testimony and describe the new person that I am becoming every day, may you also embrace the freedom, grace and redemption that Christ came for.

With love,

Christina

REBUILT: Beginning the Ending

Introduction: Beginning the Ending

Sometimes you have to begin with a blank document. In all of that, we never know what to do. But this is exactly the place that God wants us. For in this place it gives Him full rights, full access and full permission to do what He does best! In all my life, I needed control. Why? Because I lost control at a very early age in life. A broken family and a broken home only became a broken me. So I worked really hard at building ME! A part that would try to be inhumane. A part that would resist all humanity. A part that would protect myself. But all of this doesn't even make sense to what God does in life.

Even in coming to God I didn't see all of this. I didn't understand that He was the maker –the taker and the breaker… so that He could do the building and not me! That God would be the one to put in place piece by piece all things by His will and according to His perfect plan.

My plans failed…ALWAYS!

But His plans for my life have prevailed. And I gave in. 100% at all costs. Now I know for sure that this life was never my own. So here I am today, "beginning the ending" of what was the perfect storm and the perfect mess of a life so that God could get the glory. I made too many mistakes. And people reading this will be ashamed, upset, embarrassed, hurt, angry and frustrated with the decisions I MADE! Yes, I felt all of that too, believe me…But what I did find was a God that would renew, restore and rebuild a better me. His grace took away my shame. His stripes have bared all my pain. His blood was shed for my sin. And the vail was torn in two for my behalf. I have been brought near and have crossed over. I am not ashamed. I walk with my head held high because when I fell several times, God pulled me up.

I cheated on my God! I cheated on my husband! I cheated on my family! I cheated at everything that was ever handed down to me. I always wanted to do what was best for me and not for others. Yet everything I did just made me the biggest failure. Until God said to me in every way, "THIS MUST COME TO AN END!" I needed God to help me. I needed God to rescue me.

This was "beginning the ending" of my own life. Now it is a life that I live fully surrendered. What a difficult task to keep denying myself, but as I continued to see things fall into place the right way, then joy replaced my pain, tears were replaced with laughter and all fear was replaced with love.

Introduction: Beginning the Ending

Beyond recovery is the life that I live now. It took a lot to get here. But I am here. I love it. And most importantly this lowly woman has been made free indeed. I celebrate the victory that God has done in my life. When the enemy tries to strike me, I go to the one source that I had previously neglected…

GOD!

That is more than enough for me.

Thank You God. For You are my support. Thank You for Your love! Thank You for Your covering.

Without any of that, I would still be nothing. But You saw me when no one else would… ETERNALLY grateful I am. So that is why I write these words. To give YOU the glory. In this book you will find a series of writings that were the "beginning of my ending." The old Christina died so that Christ in me could live. I am a brand new creature in Christ. A whole new Christina.

Set free and delivered.

> ***"Old things** are **passed away**; behold, all **things** are become new…"* 2 Corinthians 5:17 (King James Version)

All definitions are taken from the website www.Dictionary.Com

RENEW

To begin or take up again; to make effective for an additional period; Restore to a former state;
Begin again;
Breathe new life into;
Bring up to date;
To continue;
Fix up;
Mend;
Reaffirm;
Reawaken;
Recondition;
Recreate;
Reestablish;
Refit;
Refresh;
Regenerate;
Rehabilitate;
Reinvigorate;
Remodel;
Renovate;
Reopen;
Repair;
Replenish;
Restate;
Restock;
Restore;
Revitalize;
Revive;
Stimulate;
Transform (Change Thoroughly).

PIECE 1

YOU SURVIVED

I wish that I could tell you that it was going to be easy. That your process of survival, renewal and healing would happen overnight or that it would be a cinch! But that is not the case. It is not easy to bounce back from a place that has caused severe wounds such as breaking ungodly soul ties, overcoming a divorce, the loss of a loved one in any capacity, overcoming sickness and abandonment, betrayal, addiction, depression, co-dependencies, or any other experiences that have taken up deep places in your soul.

Unfortunately, the process of healing is actually long, stressful and sometimes very painful. I could tell you what everyone needs to hear, that you will experience a rebirth and a point of peace that you never thought would be possible. Through God, certainly you will overcome. It just takes a whole lot of giving to God. It takes disciplined time and an ardent pace to get to a steady journey on your way to health and wholeness. It takes prayer, fasting, study of the word, worship, consistent church attendance, fellowship, friendship, counseling, listening to godly and spirit filled music, sermons, hobbies, work, travel, exercise and so many other rich and positive avenues that will take you to a higher and stronger walk with God. Whatever it takes for you, just understand that most probably it will be *unique* for you. Every case is different. Some people don't require all that and they have strong coping mechanisms but for others that have passed through heavy storms will definitely need a lot of help and encouragement along the way.

This book is geared to go to the one that is struggling, to the one that is asking for MORE help, to the one who keeps questioning their process, to the one who is uncertain and to the one that can't find that point of peace yet. God is it for sure and in every way but you will need to use *all the tools* that He has given you in life to get to your own wholeness. Many people aren't aware of all these things. They really don't know how. I hear this all the time, "But tell me how!" Only because I asked the same question myself.

Just know that it is YOUR process. You do not need to explain that to everyone because not everyone is going to understand YOUR process. Whatever you have to do to receive healing and wholeness has got to be done regardless of the opinions and thoughts of others. Be free in that—please! At this point in your life, it is about pleasing God and getting to a place where you are stronger and able to stand valiantly.

> *"For the weapons of our warfare are not carnal but mighty in God for pulling down strongholds, casting down arguments and every high thing that exalts itself against the knowledge of God, bringing every thought into captivity to the obedience of Christ, and being ready to punish all disobedience when your obedience is fulfilled."* 2 Corinthians 10:4-6 (NKJV)

The first question that runs through the mind during or after a tremendous trial is "How?"

How can I overcome? How long do I have to go through this? When is it going to end? How can I erase the thoughts? How can I get past the memory? How do I correct this monster of a mess? What do I do now? Don't you wish it were that simple to just take a huge eraser and start smearing everything away…even then there is still a rubbed mark left behind! There is always some *residue* left behind from any type of storm. Now it is time for God to teach you, and guide you on what to do with the remaining residue. This is the healing process. This is where the journey really begins. Those things are the natural chain of events caused by life's consequences and choices. Some of it is even results from living a sinful lifestyle. We have to take accountability for our actions.

Ask God, "Take me to the place of the supernatural where I can fully overcome what is lingering here in the natural." I heard this statement watching the movie Furious 7, "How do you kill a shadow? You shine a little light on it!" It is time for us to shine the Light of God over our circumstance this day and every day forth! With God, all things are possible and we have to believe that our healing is too.

THE TRUE BOOK...

For me I can say that God provoked me to be that open book. He wanted me to be transparent, which was never the case. In all my years, I thought I had it together. To keep the image, you have to fit this protocol. As a leader in the church, in my home, at work and in my community. Everywhere I went, it was noticeable. The day I thought I would never break—I BROKE! And I broke badly. I broke repeatedly. I wanted to know why. Because I always had some leak and residue that I could not get rid of. God literally yelled, "ENOUGH!" What looked like it was going to be a start to an amazing new year was the year I thought I would never get through.

I could honestly say that I have always suffered with some form of depression. In this particular case I ended up having a nervous breakdown. Yes, I read all the symptoms and I had all of them! I suffered anxiety, loss and a heartbreak that looked like it was beyond repair. I built my life and strength upon me and my ways. I was selfish. I put my trust in the hands of self and into the hands of others that I thought I could trust over the years, but that quickly fell to the ground and so did I. The intensity of my stress, sleepless nights and turmoil kept me sick. I thought I would lose my mind during all the violent screams and waging wars.

I messed up in a lot of areas in my life. Even through Christianity I would find myself struggling and being strongly pulled into a life of sin and stain. I can share that because I am free. I came to a point where I no longer wanted to have my family. I no longer wanted to be married to the man God gave me. I didn't want to be a mother. I didn't want to be a leader in the church. I didn't want to be anywhere near home. I didn't want to work. I wanted to leave it all.

And for what? Sounds like the perfect plan from Satan, right? Always trying to get you to leave the place where you belong. He always attacks that identity!

One day I had prayed in the sanctuary. I asked for a friend to help me get through all the rough patches of life, for God took all the real ones away. My best friend and cousin passed away. My friends moved away. My mentors left. We were the only ones left as everyone was moving on to bigger and better things. There was nothing substantial for me that I could hold onto. I became lost in my own thoughts and in the mess of my mind. I wanted to be rescued from a place of solitude. Until I found a friend but a dangerous one that would take my soul and purpose in every other direction that was away from my original calling. I became lost. And I wanted to die. I thought that nothing else could take away the pain I felt.

In the beginning of 2015 --January, my husband called me and recognized that I was sliding into a world of sin. He pulled everything from me and told me that if I would not change, everything would be over. I ran away from home! It was the coldest night ever. I stood by myself in a hotel and cried myself to sleep. I answered calls from no one. I threw the entire home into an uproar. After much attempts I answered and he asked me to come back home. He wanted me to know that home was our home. That we would decide together and for our family. I harkened, came back to a broken, angry and hurt family. But they received me. They wanted me home—just like this. The same way that God did. I saw CHRIST IN THEM. I fought through the tears, shame and pain.

By the beginning of February, I was scheduled to speak at a retreat. I couldn't speak this way. This was my surrendering. It was a very humiliating and humbling position to be in but I did it. I wanted a change, I DID. I came to another dark place and I began to document everything that God was doing in me. It was part of my healing. I had felt like King Nebuchadnezzar.

The Dream Is Fulfilled

All this happened to King Nebuchadnezzar. Twelve months later, as the king was walking on the roof of the royal palace of Babylon, he said, "Is not this the great Babylon I have built as the royal residence, by my mighty power and for the glory of my majesty?" Even as the words were on his lips, a voice came from heaven, "This is what is decreed for you, King Nebuchadnezzar: Your royal **authority has been taken from you.** You will be driven away from people and will live with the wild animals; you will eat grass like the ox. Seven times will pass by for you until you acknowledge that the Most High is sovereign over all kingdoms on earth and gives them to anyone he wishes." Immediately what had been said about Nebuchadnezzar was fulfilled. He was driven away from people and ate grass like the ox. His body was drenched with the dew of heaven until his hair grew like the feathers of an eagle and his nails like the claws of a bird. At the end of that time, I, Nebuchadnezzar, raised my eyes toward heaven, and **my sanity was restored**. Then I praised the Most High; I honored and glorified him who lives forever.

His dominion is an eternal dominion;
his kingdom endures from generation to generation.
All the peoples of the earth
 are regarded as nothing.
He does as he pleases
 with the powers of heaven
 and the peoples of the earth.
No one can hold back his hand
 or say to him: "What have you done?"

At the same time that my sanity was restored, my honor and splendor were returned to me for the glory of my kingdom. My advisers and nobles sought me out, and I was restored to my throne and became even greater than before. Now I, Nebuchadnezzar, praise and exalt and glorify the King of heaven, because everything he does is right and all his ways are just. And those who walk in pride he is able to humble. Daniel 4:28-37 (New International Version)

This was me. In a nutshell I was a hotheaded leader that needed to be put in place and yield to God. It is a hurting place but one of healing.

I remember walking back to my counselor's office broken, tattered and torn. Everything was so dark and desolate, so I shared that with him when I could not speak most days. He listened to me expose my thoughts and a lot of things I have done, many of which I am not proud of and suffered for. I will never forget any of the words that he said to me especially on that day. I was having a hard time coping with serious situations and everything inside me was destroyed. This is what he said:

"Control your feelings
But don't deny them
You are human
Give yourself room for redemption
Because we ALL need it!"

I walked out of that room feeling like such a weight was lifted off my chest. It was only the beginning stage of reaching a place of brokenness. Then there is the point where I was severely broken. This was the point of no return. I came to realize that all my study, titles and accumulative resources never sustained me. What keeps you sustained is the very presence of God, coupled with prayer and study—it is a must.

Sometimes we forget what Jesus Christ did for all humanity. He died for ALL of our sins which will encompass past, present and future. He took our burdens to the cross and our sickness and shame. Isn't that what the word declares? That is why Jesus said on the cross "It is finished" in John 19:30. As humans, we typically see from a limited capacity and not from a spiritual and biblical perspective. God sent His one and only Son for this purpose.

> *"Surely He has borne our griefs And carried our sorrows; Yet we esteemed Him stricken, Smitten by God, and afflicted. But He was wounded for our transgressions, He was bruised for our iniquities; The chastisement for our peace was upon Him, And by His stripes we are healed. All we like sheep have gone astray; We have turned, every one, to his own way; And the Lord has laid on Him the iniquity of us all."* Isaiah 53:4-6 (New King James Version)

I took communion at a church and I remember still thinking about the things I had done wrong. Then they put an image of Jesus Christ going to the cross. I sat in my seat with the cup and bread with uncontrollable tears. I had the most intimate moment with God at that point. I knew in my mind that as humans, we will always think the worst but we have to know the best. That is what Jesus did for us. He redeemed me. He redeemed us all. I am no different from any person across this earth. We are all flesh beings in need of a savior.

> *For EVERYONE has sinned; we all fall short of God's glorious standards.* Romans 3:23 (New Living Translation)

That is our nature and we need that redemption. Let's stop focusing on everything that we have done and focus on the one thing that He did right. He redeemed us!

Perhaps someone at this very moment needs to hear this right now. Stop beating yourself up for things you have done wrong or things that went awry. Stop beating others up for their things as well. We need a heart that embraces redemption. A heart that forgives because it costs us more pain to hold on to sin and shame.

If God did it for me, He does it for all. Give yourself and others room for redemption.

You survived all of this, now you are alive and can live to thrive in all that you do. Freedom is absolutely beautiful.

PIECE 2

I'M BACKWARDS

*Sometimes you have to walk backwards,
but don't worry because you are still moving!*

I have come to realize that everyone has "skeletons in their closet." There are many people that seem to be off. Like they do nothing right. Everything they try just comes to ruins. It is not just me. Everyone has a past. Everyone has a history. And everyone certainly isn't perfect, that is why we need a perfect Savior.

I always thought about me and kept myself in a selfish bubble because I didn't know how to deal with trauma. Until God actually stripped me down to the bare bone to see the skeletons! I was walking in the street in hysteria and cried out, "GOD! Help me. I'm in an extremely wounded condition here! I am severely broken, depressed, sad, frustrated, angry, I feel so powerless. Everything is stripped from me, I have nothing! I feel nothing. I'm completely numb here. I'm in the most devastating state of pain and anguish. I'm asking you if these bones can live?!?"

The beginning stages of recovery are always going feel like a bad dream or nightmare that you can't wake up from. Recovery is not just about getting up from being broken but it is about getting up because we are SEVERELY broken!

> *"But You have severely broken us in the place of jackals, and covered us with the shadow of death."* Psalm 44:19 (New King James Version)

Some days are just better than other days and we have to take them one at a time. Nothing can change that or the way we feel about them. It is irrelevant. It is called our unique process. That will vary for each person. Your process is your own. When I know I am moving forward but it feels like I am still going backwards I have to remind myself. My mind has this constant war that goes backwards. I keep replaying things over and over. I think about everything at once and I try to get past that.

I stood in a sad place again when I know I did what God wanted me to do but my soulish realm was begging for immediate comfort. The only comfort for me would be reaching out. I decided to text a friend and told her my struggle. I can't do this alone. She wrote me back –to get a hold of myself, to think of my family and that I would have to be my own motivator now until everything else gets into shape.

"Lean on the Lord! He is sufficient enough for you my friend!"

To me that was like a shout. I searched through the internet for relevant scripture and came to this passage:

> "But sin, taking opportunity by the commandment, produced in me all manner of evil desire. For apart from the law sin was dead. I was alive once without the law, but when the commandment came, sin revived and I died. And the commandment, which was to bring life, I found to bring death. For sin, taking occasion by the commandment, deceived me, and by it killed me. Therefore the law is holy, and the commandment holy and just and good. Has then what is good become death to me? Certainly not! But sin, that it might appear sin, was producing death in me through what is good, so that sin through the commandment might become exceedingly sinful. For we know that the law is spiritual, but I am carnal, sold under sin. For what I am doing, I do not understand. For what I will to do, that I do not practice; but what I hate, that I do. If, then, I do what I will not to do, I agree with the law that it is good. But now, it is no longer I who do it, but sin that dwells in me. For I know that in me (that is, in my flesh) nothing good dwells; for to will is present with me, but how to perform what is good I do not find. For the good that I will to do, I do not do; but the evil I will not to do, that I practice. Now if I do what I will not to do, it is no longer I who do it, but sin that dwells in me. I find then a law, that evil is present with me, the

one who wills to do good. For I delight in the law of God according to the inward man. But I see another law in my members, warring against the law of my mind, and bringing me into captivity to the law of sin which is in my members. O wretched man that I am! Who will deliver me from this body of death? I thank God—through Jesus Christ our Lord! So then, with the mind I myself serve the law of God, but with the flesh the law of sin." Romans 7:8-25 (New King James Version)

There is a time for everything in its season. There is a time to ask for help and there is a time that you will be more independent. That is simply up to you and where you find yourself at the moment. We constantly have to be in a place where we can take this self-assessment and say "Am I okay to do this alone? What help do I really need?"

I went strong in prayer one day. I cried out and I cried out! God did show me that person I could trust during this time. Other times, He shows me His word. I can feel when the spirit brings me to a serene place. I just have to stay there and rest on Him in my time of prayer. Other times it is in worship and songs. The lyrics speak for me when I have no words.

When I read Romans 7, I was sitting in a nail salon waiting to be next. I wept as I felt this word pierce my heart. I hated to be in a place of pain again. But I loved how God was moving in my soul—He was cleaning, washing and moving in it. Perhaps Paul found himself constantly in a place where he felt like he was going back…just like I felt it and like you feel it too. This place will be a breathing ground to start again- God's way! Think of that moment when he was Saul—knocked off of his horse on his way to Damascus. He needed to be renewed.

Reminder…tell yourself, "BE CALM! Just be calm!" Just because it looks like we are going in the opposite direction doesn't mean we are going the wrong way. Noel Clark said, "You have to climb down from the mountain you took yourself to." This was the first step. This is progress! This is healing. We have to visit these places of pain to take it out, over a span of time so that we allow ourselves room to cry, mourn or grieve. This is how we learn that it is not about us. It is not what always makes the most sense. It is about being in a complete submission and surrender unto God. It is as our friend and apostle Femi Adun says, "Submerge so that you can emerge." In this our roots will be so deep in Him. We actually become immovable. It is a relationship that will now be built stronger than any other.

We need to come to a point where we become transparent. It is okay to be "backwards" God is a fixer and this transparency is good for you. It is a place where we can easily recognize that we need saving.

You don't have to be closed in. You are not a statue or a stone. You are human. You are real. You have a heartbeat and sometimes just like everyone else…it aches! It is okay to be real. It is OKAY to seek that which will make you stronger when you need it the most.

I am so thankful that God put in my life very positive and spirit-filled people. They accept me and love me with open arms always. There are no conditions on the love that they have for me and that is why I am not ashamed to call them F A M I L Y! But in all of this I have learned so much within the last year with some pressing trials in my life…. There is more!

I am a wife, a mother, a full-time worker, a pastor, a leader, a teacher and I wear all these hats. I would nicely state that I am someone that still needs lifting. I had actively seen a professional counselor for two years. Coming back to New York from that retreat in Florida, I recognized I still needed more. I needed transparency. I needed a renewal and an awakening within me. It was a place where I could take off the mask and put on the mantle. God wanted me to let down all the walls so that He could reveal all the things He had for me.

An amazing relationship with GOD.

A family that loves me unconditionally.

An ability and a gift that keeps me alive and moving in the Body of Christ.

A body of sisterhood among my church that is really blossoming into a powerful women's ministry.

A newfound passion to revive that hidden talent in me for a continual renewal in my life.

A consistent relationship with mentors that bring me wise counsel.

A strive for activities that will keep me focused to do all this and more.

In all of this, I can say that this experience has been life changing. From the moment I had an encounter with God to the moment I came back to my role at home, work and church. I had to recognize that when I need help, I simply need to ask for it and from the right people God has placed in my life. They are there and always have been. We just become so stuck behind this wall that we cannot see the truth until all the walls come tumbling down… Then you can see life a whole lot clearer. Thank you God for tearing down all the walls in my life. You came to my rescue to destroy what was always trying to destroy me.

The words of my counselor Clark are always ringing through my ears. He stood reminding me during those teary sessions— "There are pastors that preach the word of God and pastors that live the word of God." This was part of my experience sitting in the pews and not just standing in the pulpit, where I can feel what the people feel. I am a part of a body that may look backwards to many but they are so blessed in Christ. He makes the crooked straight. He makes the broken whole. He makes the lesser greater.

I am thankful to my family and friends for being there for me. They are helping me to get through all the dark days and celebrating with me in the days where there is light. And even if I shed those tears, there is always that one that catches them and smiles right back at me saying, "YOU GOT THIS CHRIS… you GOT this!" That makes this process of renewal so much more worthwhile. It is where I get to realize that there is hope for me. I don't have to remain in the darkest pit of turmoil. God is getting me out of there completely.

The complete part happens when we yield to Him. Through experiencing that backwards motion, I learned how to fall forward in the hands of God! You will lose a lot of things during this process but many of which never belonged there in the first place. If people walk out of your life, it only means they weren't meant to be there. All things remaining, is what God will use to begin a new work in you and you will find that to be more worthwhile, wholesome and lasting.

There is a world of wonders out there waiting for us to explore. If we were hurt in one place, doesn't mean that we will hurt in every place. There is a place that we will grow and a place that we can flourish. You will find it!

> ***The earth is the Lord's, and all its fullness, The world and those who dwell therein.*** Psalm 24:1 (New King James Version)

PIECE 3
MY PERFECT STORM

I received a daily devotional email entitled, "An Unexpected Storm" which was driven off a book written by James Merritt, "52 Weeks with Jesus". He goes to describe the scene of the storm out of Mark 4: 36-40 as it states:

> Leaving the crowd, they took Him with them, in the boat, just as He was. And other boats were with Him. And a great windstorm arose and the waves were breaking into the boat, so that the boat was already filling. But He was in the stern, asleep on the cushion. And they woke Him and said to Him, "Teacher, do you not care that we are perishing?" and He awoke and rebuked the wind and said to the sea, "Peace! Be still!" And the wind ceases and there was a great calm. He said to them, "Why are you so afraid? Have you still no faith?"

What really caught my attention was the closing statement "He will calm the tempest after it has served its purpose."

I asked myself, "Did my storm serve its purpose yet? Is that why it is not yet calm? Is that why it has not yet ceased at this time?"

I struggled with that because although the storm has stopped on the outside for the most part, I don't feel calm inside! In fact, I feel quite stirred up most days and find that it is taking such huge effort to bring myself to a place of stability, comfort and calmness. I preach the word, minister words of life and when I need it most, I have to yell this over my own life repeatedly for the memory of the waves that are breaking into my boat and filling it to capacity. These waves are still daunting to me!

I want everything to be okay, to be at peace and to be well. Jesus calmed the storm but there is a bigger storm going on in the inside that no one can see but us! This is what moves us, it scares and terrifies us. How do we calm THAT piece of it...the place where no one sees? Our own haven that is being shook...it is our home, our land, our family or our friends. Sometimes it is all the things closest to us causing the shake. If we can conquer it at home than we can conquer it anywhere right? Because a part of all that external mess and garbage from the storm, there is a bigger thing happening inside of us! I personalize this message for me...

I NEED THAT CALM
A REAL CALM

Calm is without motion, still, not windy or stormy, free from excitement or passion, tranquil and freedom from disturbance! We need freedom from all those internal frictions that try to disturb us.

Don't let those things disrupt you. It will get better, it will! I have to speak that to myself. I want to be free from the negative excitement and all that stirs in me the pain, hurt and anguish.

When I was checking—it hurt like hell. Then I asked someone else to check, it hurt a little less. Then I could only assume that I won't ask anyone else next but only God to check! Check on that God. Please keep it in perfect peace, bliss, joy, grace...for that is the blessing in my understanding! Then I know that I got that peace down packed where God is the source of my strength. I need sisterhood. I need gatherings and fellowship. I need church. There's a freedom when I worship the King of kings.

When I preach, life is brushed back into my bones and my spirit is no longer overwhelmed...but I'm not in this place 24-7. My world comes down...its cessation will be reached and I know I am in the place called home. Alone...in my mind...where now it is just ME, MY MIND and God. I hear that preaching over and over from the last 7 words that ring in my ears, "My God, My God...why have You forsaken me?" I felt forsaken and forgotten. I felt forsaken when I was laughed at, yes even by friends. I felt forsaken when no one reached out to me. I felt forsaken when people I knew closely were giving me cruel looks. I felt forsaken when people didn't even want to approach or greet me. I felt like there was nothing or no one left. Like no one could ever come close or fill the void but I know that God can. I trust that God can. I believe that God can! I just know that I know…

So this is where I have MY perfect storm. The disciples shouted with all their might, "JESUS… WAKE UP! WE ARE PERISHING! WE ARE DROWNING!"

Don't you ever feel like you are drowning?

Don't you ever feel like the rain won't stop?

Don't you ever feel like the storm won't cease?

Don't you ever feel like that gnawing feeling won't ever go away?

Don't you ever feel like you won't ever find that permanent peace?

When we KNOW it exists… we KNOW God exists… We know He is in the same boat with us! He was human right? He was live in the flesh so He felt everything we felt. How torn He must have felt when Judas came and kissed his cheek. How torn He must have felt when all the disciples fled. How torn He must have felt to hear Peter who swore repeatedly that he would never leave him curse the people away and say that he **NEVER KNEW JESUS!**

So when I think of my storm… that seems like the BEST… the PERFECT problem… the PERFECT one and the only one… I have to know it is yet one thing in the eyes of God that He took on the cross of Calvary by the way of Jesus. How much more PERFECT IS THAT? My perfect storm will never be in comparison to that of Jesus Christ.

When we feel that boat breaking from the storm, it will serve its purpose and glorify God.

REBUILT: Beginning the Ending

PIECE 4

REBOOT – SYSTEM PROCESSING

Anything that reminds you of the pain, you have to change, delete and remove.

Recovery is hard. Let's consider the computer fix situation. That is probably the best way I can describe me at this state. On a better day, I decided when I got out of bed that I needed a conquest. I decided to shower and finally do my hair. I was walking around like a zombie for months and I didn't think anyone really noticed that much except me. Only because I would always get finely dressed and dolled up. I had energy for the gym and energy to get in a place where I wanted to be recognized. Now it was quite the contrary. I didn't want to be seen. I didn't want anyone to notice me and I was not up for talking most days even though my line of business required much talking.

I was still in some form of an aftershock after all my issues came to the light. As things were being removed from me, I still found it very difficult to find a stable coping mechanism and a source of strength – even though I knew that is God. I am talking about the mind thing that was impacting the heart thing, that was impacting the physical thing! Thus, leaving me with depleted energy. I cried in the gym when I tried to work out. I had no strength. This doesn't really sound encouraging right, but it is the truth. I wallowed for a long time. I was having the ultimate break down

I coach myself, "It is my day – TODAY!" Everyone mainly writes about the overcoming piece, they found the answer and the struggle is over, but is that ever the case? Where is that for me and my current situation? When the struggle grew worse. Is this the point of processing and rebooting so I can experience restoration? I asked God, "When is this going to go away? When will I not feel this haunting and agonizing pain? When will I stop crying?" My eyes would always look swollen and would hurt. I know the day will come but it is not my day yet. I know I am not the only one…especially as it is written in the word repeatedly by one of the greatest leaders of all, King David!

> ***I cried to the LORD with my voice, And He heard me from His holy hill.*** Psalm 3:4 (New King James Version)

> ***In my distress I called upon the LORD, And cried out to my God; He heard my voice from His temple, And my cry came before Him, even to His ears.*** Psalm 18:6 (New King James Version)

> ***I cried out to God with my voice—To God with my***

voice; And He gave ear to me. Psalm 77:1 (New King James Version)

In my distress I cried unto the LORD, and He heard me. Psalm 120:1 (New King James Version)

David was doing a whole lot of crying! For a man, I don't think this is very common but it is recorded for our history and understanding. IT IS OKAY TO CRY OUT! God listens to us and for as long as it takes, He will provide to us the help! Do we even understand how difficult it is to cope, to forget things, to move on, to renew the mind and be rebuilt? This takes aggressive work. This is the process. At the time we come to realize this, we can put up our sign "System Processing! I am a work in progress!"

I had several computer switches in my house and have come to the conclusion that we function just like these computers. I analyzed the whole process of setting up the new computer and cleaning out the old ones. Each in itself was its own process. I was switching from a MacBook Pro to a Lenovo laptop. These are two different operating systems that were both very complex when it came to cleaning and setting up. The first issue was exceeding all available space on the MacBook Pro. I had tried as much as I could to clean it out bit by bit but I was too close to the 500 Gig capacity no matter how much I tried to delete. Especially having to make the choice of what to keep and what to get rid of. If I wanted the computer to be restored and to function better before handing it over to another user, I would have to wipe the memory as clean as I could. I had to buy an external drive, another tool to wipe the computer and start to tackle this lengthy process. All the while doing this I thought of my spiritual, mental and emotional state. I was also undergoing a lengthy process of restoration. I wish it was that easy to DELETE things in my life. Things I have done, things I was experiencing and come to a point where I can delete the memories that continued to haunt me during the process.

Just as the word declares, this is a work in progress and a continual effort on our behalf. The first stage is actually just placing your life before God!

> *"So here's what I want you to do, God helping you: Take your everyday, ordinary life—your sleeping, eating, going-to-work, and walking-around life—and place it before God as an offering. Embracing what God does for you is the best thing you can do for him. Don't become so well-adjusted to your culture that you fit into it without even thinking. Instead, fix your attention on God. You'll be changed from the inside out. Readily recognize what he wants from you, and quickly respond to it. Unlike the culture around you, always dragging you down to its level of immaturity, God brings the best out of you, develops well-formed maturity in you."* Romans 12:1-2 (The Message)

I have to place my life before God every single day and recognize what He wants me to do. It is no longer that I live a selfish life I can no longer say what I want to say, do what I want to do and go where I want to go. My life has to be under full submission and I have to say what He wants

Reboot – System Processing

me to say, do what He wants me to do and go where He wants me to go.

As I continued to work on the Macbook, it became frustrating trying to figure out how to clean up all the clutter. I found that as I was actually deleting everything by moving it to the trash, then I had to click "Empty Trash" and even then I could see that it was not removed off the hard drive. I had to purchase a tool called "**Omni** Disc Sweeper". What an unusual tool but it worked! The files I deleted moved to another space on the drive into a place called "Other". Our "Omni-Disc Sweeper" is our "Omni-Potent" God who is all powerful. We seek Him more. He sent the Holy Spirit to sweep us clean from all our past pains.

> "Your past is no longer a place of *pain*. It is a place of *grace*." Femi Adun

Isn't that funny how our life works like this. We want to delete everything and just do a reboot! It is hard for our system to process what is actually happening to us when God is trying to clean us up! As much as we try to remove, reframe, resist and delete we still have an ongoing battle even after making the firm decision to follow God wholeheartedly! No matter how many retreats we go on or how many power filled services, we will always come back to our real life! Nothing goes away just like that. It takes work, time, effort and a deeper cleansing of the soul. Which is part of the healing process. It is a whole new lifestyle.

You have to try to keep the mind pure, the thoughts run

rampant as you are constantly being bombarded with memories and it hurts! It hurts so much. As you are there reading, praying, writing, getting therapy and trying to stay as filled as you can, the memories are going to come and haunt you like a flood! They are constant and you have to ask God for the utmost help in keeping your mind sane and focused during these times. You must understand that you have to give your mind time to adjust to the new things that you are now depositing in it!

Rebooting is giving your heart! Starting fresh! Starting over!

Deleting is getting rid of all the things that no longer belong in the space of your mind!

If pain is tied to it—remove it! What are you keeping it for? Why nuture something painful? Why keep feeding the pain rather than starving it? Try nuturing something useful, real and more beneficial for you. It is time to create new memories.

This is the "Be Ye Renewed" concept in Ephesians 5. We have so many things to hold on to that will keep us focused. The most effective source has got to be the Word. It has to work, it has to govern our every move now and the day will come when the rest will pass.

> ***"For our light affliction, which is but for a moment, is working for us a far more exceeding and eternal weight of glory."*** 2 Corinthians 4:17 (New King James Version)

"And do not be conformed to this world, but be transformed by the renewing of your mind, that you may prove what is that good and acceptable and perfect will of God." Romans 12:2 (New King James Version)

"Casting down arguments and every high thing that exalts itself against the knowledge of God, bringing every thought into captivity to the obedience of Christ." 2 Corinthians 10:5 (New King James Version)

Get rid of it! All of it. Anything that tries to bring you down or entertain your past – just trash. As the thoughts come, you have to cast them down. Talk it out. Think of something else. Focus on something better or you will end up back in the largest pity party of all.

This is what you have to meditate on now and that is a training in itself.

<u>Meditate on These Things</u>

"Finally, brethren, whatever things are true, whatever things are noble, whatever things are just, whatever things are pure, whatever things are lovely, whatever things are of good report, if there is any virtue and if there is anything praiseworthy—meditate on these things." Philippians 4:8 (New King James Version)

That is a whole list of things to meditate on. What we have to do is **replace** the lies with the truth of God's Word. What we think is lovely is not so lovely in the eyes of God. We need to come to a position where we confess those things before God and experience a real repentance so that our restoration will begin. It hurts because we thought it was true, we thought it was noble, we throught it was right, we thought it was the purest thing, we thought it was lovely, and that it was good for us. Yet, we are actually wrong for anything that leads to a life of sin and leads us down to a road of death.

So our experience of death should be when we rid of all that is sin and all that is false. We can no longer do things our way. They must be God's way.

Then breathe, because now we are doing the right thing!

This is all a factor stemming from what we choose to hold on to in our memory banks. Our minds fall under attack with our memory. Forgetting is the hardest part when you have already let go. Somewhere in the mind, there is a record kept. It pops up every so often. We have this memory bank that is alive and well. There are pros and cons with having this as part of our being.

We need to hold onto good things, retain positive moments, a history of success, encouraging memories, knowledge and more. But the memories that are unpleasant we have to work to discard. Those are the memories that you need to delete completely. If they were pleasant yet you had to move forward by letting go, start by creating something better.

Letting go doesn't happen in a moment—it happens with consistency!

We would like to forget only because we don't like to feel like we are missing something huge in our life that is now gone. It would be nice to forget. Why feel such a loss like that? Yet why is it so hard for us to forget? Easier said than done because it takes so much effort. It is not an easy thing to inadvertently neglect, to attend to, or mention something of great significance. It is not an easy thing to put out of one's mind; to cease to think of or consider when they are matters of the heart.

The Word of God tells us to FORGET! Just FORGET! Neglect! Don't mention! Put it out of your mind!

> *Not that I have already obtained all this, or have already arrived at my goal, but I press on to take hold of that for which Christ Jesus took hold of me. Brothers and sisters, I do not consider myself yet to have taken hold of it. But one thing I do: Forgetting what is behind and straining toward what is ahead, I press on toward the goal to win the prize for which God has called me heavenward in Christ Jesus. All of us, then, who are mature should take such a view of things. And if on some point you think differently, that too God will make clear to you.* Philippians 3:12-15 (New International Version)

Yet we are caught in these two worlds of past and present. Should we forget good things?

Even if they are good—they are in the past and we have to spend more time mentally on the FUTURE. Many times we become prisoners of our past. Just because some memories were good, we have to accept that they are GONE! For some situations we all experience going through some sort of grieving process. Family or friends move away, we move away, relationships end, school is complete, companies close, people pass away, animals are gone and children grow up and then they move out... all these things are part of the life cycle. A constant motion is always happening, yet sometimes our minds get STUCK in a particular place! Some will think – "But what if that is all I have left? What if it was something tragic that is hard to shake off? How do we move on successfully and fruitfully?"

BUILD NEW MEMORIES

This is the time where we clean up our memory bank with new resources. Try collecting new things and put your focus on that. Moving ahead. Moving forward. Living in the present. Living for your future. An eternal life is waiting for you, not a past life. It is a constant effort and constant work as part of our daily renewal and growth. Even when it seems impossible to move forward, know that God will do it. When you don't see a road, He will make one!

> ***Behold, I will do a new thing, now it shall spring forth; Shall you not know it? I will even make a road in the wilderness and rivers in the desert.*** Isaiah 43:19 (New King James Version)

With Christ in our life, He makes all things new. It is our promise. This is our emphasis now. New things and a new focus.

Don't live in the place of "yester-years." Now we have a new time to create something worthwhile. So when your past beckons you to wallow in it – just do something different for yourself to make a new memory bank filled with God's precious promises. When your mind runs into that moment and shouts, "Don't Forget!" Well… we have to remember that God's word tells us to forget those things behind us.

Reboot! Allow your internal system to process the new things that God wants to do with you.

REBUILT: Beginning the Ending

PIECE 5

HOW LONG

This is the first thing many have asked! We keep finding ourselves a lot of times in this walk asking the same, "How long". Honestly, how long is the "how long" stage? How long do I have to go through this? How long does the grieving continue? When does the pain go away? When does the healing really take place? When do the tears actually stop? When will my circumstance change? This seems endless. I am tired! Tired! Tired!

At least we know on this earth there was a man that adequately described this for our learning.

> *How long, O Lord? Will You forget me forever? How long, will You hide Your face from me? How long shall I take counsel in my soul, having sorrow in my heart DAILY? How long will my enemy be exalted over me? Consider and hear me, O Lord my God; enlighten my eyes, Lest I sleep the sleep of death; Lest my enemy say,*

> *"I have prevailed against him"; Lest those who trouble me rejoice when I am moved. But I have trusted in Your mercy; My heart shall rejoice in Your salvation. I will sing to the Lord, because He has dealt bountifully with me.* Psalm 13 (New King James Version)

So how long does it take? As long as it takes for you to continually take comfort in God. For the healing and victory, it will actually take EVERY DAY... that is your answer. It is a dedication and commitment to God that you must give to Him daily. For daily you messed up and tried to do everything your way, right? So daily you must do things His way.

We have to continue through our journey! As much as we struggle to conform to flesh... We must continue to transform through His Word! DAILY! I bet you thought you were the only one. No, there will be others worse than your case but DAILY we **all** must fight through the struggle! Remember that we have to pick the FIGHT! The Bible declares....

> *"And Jonathan attacked the garrison of the Philistines that was in Geba, and the Philistines heard of it. Then Saul blew the trumpet throughout all the land, saying, "Let the Hebrews hear!"* I Samuel 13:3 (New King James Version)

Every day is a new opportunity for us to do something amazing. Go after something greater. Find it in God, in His word, inspirational books, music, fellowship and more. Whatever will take you to a better positive place –go through it.

Smile that you had an experience.

Smile that you will have even more.

Go through your training—not just to fight but to make a difference and be a person of special influence. Put on that armor of God and fight through every season. Nothing in life comes easy. And your renewal and recovery will not be easy either. It is a great effort that you will need to choose to pursue. In any stage of something whether it be the beginning, the middle or the end, we still have to be fierce about it to succeed. Jonathan knew the battle to pick. We can choose those too. We don't have to bring ourselves to the same type of battle. FIGHT that off, there is more in life to get to higher places. The effort you put in is necessary and will not go unseen or unrewarded. You will make a difference.

How long will all this take to pass through your journey? Every day forward, we keep building for a new and brighter future.

In order to get something new you have to move away from that past! PACK THOSE BAGS UP AND LET THE PROCESS begin. No more delays, pit stops or hindrances on the journey.

Move Mentally – Move Physically.

As time is flying by you will see how dynamic and life changing your life is becoming. God can change your location, position or many other factors. All that will happen as it is required.

I had experienced that type of change too. I was so excited. I knew that God was going to be changing a lot more things and I was ready for this move. I moved to the city as part of my career and I know God was leading me there. I needed to put the past of the previous place behind me.

You have to be ready to move on to new venues that God has. Be prepared for change.

Be ready to explore new ground.

Be ready to do whatever it takes to help press ahead.

I know packing isn't always fun either. We decide what needs to come with us and what needs to go! Sometimes we just need everything new. I keep reminding myself of this scripture:

> **Forget what happened before, And do not think about the past. Look at the new thing I am going to do. It's already happening. Don't you see it?** Isaiah 43:18-19 (New Century Version)

I see it! It is time for us to MOVE! For too long we wallow in that how long stage. We live there, foster it, feed it and keep ourselves stuck in the same issues. Some of it is good and some of it is not. We have to mentally sift through all of that and discard what needs to go. When God wants to take you some place new, He doesn't want you to keep harping on what happened before.

How Long

Think about it... What is your mind doing to help that or change that? It is impossible.

MOVE ON!

Relationships don't grow, you don't grow and things never get resolved when we keep reflecting on the past. Then we have become a prisoner of our past. We don't get out. We stay incarcerated mentally! WOW! And you have the power to change all of that if you look to what is ahead...look at what is new for you!

It may even bring you frustration—by others that are not changing. Why don't THEY change?! How long shall this continue? Honestly, the first focus should always be YOU! And that is where inner peace will reside. That is what counts the most.

Are you changing?

God has amazing things coming down the pike! He says, "Look there! Look at the new thing!" Stop focusing on what is NOT changing and focus on WHAT IS changing! Let that be you! He says, "It is already happening...don't you see it!"

I do! I see it, feel it, sense it, think it, live it and I LOVE IT!

I need this! And I know you need it too. It is what's best for us. I don't want to remain in a place that is stagnant. I don't want to remain in a dry land or wandering around the desert. This is the 41st year – the years next will be OUT of the wilderness. I want to be by the well. I want to never thirst again. When I bring myself to the heart of God, I see the change. I experience a new birth inside. That to me is worth this move. It is not easy but it is worth it all. Time to let go of all the past, the baggage, the anger, the resentment, the memories, the blame game, the mistakes and even all that was good– He has better things in store!

> ***The glory of this present house will be greater than the glory of the former house,' says the LORD Almighty. 'And in this place I will grant peace,' Declares the LORD Almighty."*** Haggai 2:9 (New International Version)

God promises to make the new house **GREATER**! The new place that He brings you to will be more promising! Imagine that new house is YOU. He is saying —what you have NOW in the present is GREATER than what you ever had. This will also be a place of peace! It is not farther down the road. It is not years to come. It is not a dream or a fantasy. It is what God wants to do with your house NOW!

Can you let Him?

Give it all to Him, pack your bags, get ready, keep cleaning house and making moves instead of excuses. Embrace the change. Trust that it is going to be far beyond what you could ever imagine. God is able to do it. How long will that all take? It happens the moment you embrace the change that has to happen in you first.

> ***Now all glory to God, who is able, through His mighty power at work within us, to accomplish infinitely more***

than we might ask or think. Ephesians 3:20 (New Living Translation)

Don't stagger anymore. In all that –it has never brought you peace the way a hope anchored in God could be. Change IS here. We are IN the move. As this new season approaches, let's keep pressing with a mindset that says, "I'm ready God! Take me to the place where I have that complete rest in a house that you made specifically for me. A glorious place, so much better than the former." It will be a spacious place.

This is the time–pack your bags! Because we are moving! It could be that when you get to that new place –that it is already newly and fully furnished! That's the God thing! All you ever needed to pack was you…. God provides the rest. Amen!

REBUILT: Beginning the Ending

PIECE 6

WHAT CAVE ARE YOU IN

Why have we allowed so many things to keep us in a cave? Such a stronghold to push through.

You may experience times where everything around you will be going against or contrary to your promise. Now that you have decided to pick up and leave all of your past mess behind, it will feel like no one will be on the same page as you. King David found himself in rough places where he tried to pick himself up repeatedly. He then comes to see that his true calling as an exceptional leader is just beginning. I delivered a sermon at my church on March 23, 2015 when I was feeling more positive with my progress. It was titled, "What Cave Are You In?"

I preached a new sermon, a real sermon, a now sermon and a sermon for today. It is my life. Because I live this every day and people would never think so. Our battle is constant and ongoing. As we are currently on a journey…including my own, we are reminded that this is a new lifetime walk with the Lord. This takes intentionality, courage, tremendous strength and effort.

David was a mighty warrior. Why didn't they want to follow a king like Saul? Because Saul wasn't a fighter. He was just a man with a title. David was a fighter, a warrior, had surrendered to a life of battle, continual lifetime of war and a chase until he became a CHAMPION. He was a true leader. It may not be as helpful to know about a battle that happened 20 years ago! When what we really need to know is how to handle things going on today! Help me TODAY! Saul was known over a slaughter that happened over years of past time. He also had an issue with obedience and taking out the people God asked him to as a victory. He didn't complete any God-given tasks and only man-made tasks.

People don't want to talk to others with a facade of victory or those never encountering a thing! We call this "pretenders." They don't really share about what they are encountering today. They just pretend that they have no issues and profess to live a perfect life. They also tell you never to share anything. Not to talk of any intimate issues! That you have to behave like all is well in your house, your job, with your kids, with your finances… everything must always be peachy! BY FAITH!

But you need help!

If you keep partially telling your testimony it will only partially help for healing... but when you tell your complete story...your complete testimony, then you can come to a complete breakthrough. That is typically how we help to give strength out not only to ourselves but to those that God places us in contact with. Those who are renewed can help point the way for others.

"Only one who is restored can be a restorer."
Apostle Femi Adun

"It takes a free man to free a man."
Mike Shea, New Day New Me Recovery Journal

What is the issue? People want to know HOW! How do they get out of this? Where do they go? What do they do? People need HELP! Real help! So let's get real, be authentic and start being the vessel that God ordained us to be!

If King David had his life on blast and still was a man after God's own heart what makes you an exception to the rule? David had a woman issue so much so that it carried over to his son Solomon with 1000 wives and concubines. Apostle Paul was slaughtering Christians before he was encouraging them! Apostle Peter was lying to them before he was leading them!

Let's really tell our story! You don't need to disclose all the detail to the world, but the problem can be identified. That is how we begin that healing. The detail will be provided when and if God leads you to tell it. The more you share in the right places, the more healing it can actually bring to those that need it. That is all in prayer.

Many times you don't want to open up because you think you will be HURT! NO! What ever happened - happened!

The deed is done! And by His stripes you are **healed** and by His blood you have already been **set free**! You don't have a scar from your past, you have a testimony!

YOUR SALVATION IS NOT GIVEN TO YOU BY ANY OTHER PERSON BUT JESUS HIMSELF... and THAT is eternal!

David was in the cave of Adullum. Saul was in a palace eating supper!

David went to Mizpah, Saul sought just 1 man out of jealousy and David sought hundreds and thousands because of the God he served.

Saul had an army of 300,000 of Israel and 30,000 of Judah.

David had 1 (Jonathan) until God gave him 400 men just like him as a start. They were all in distress. The world was shaken up in the city at that time. There was no order with all these "kings..." That is life. Are you okay? Because it is okay to "not be okay" when you do find yourself in that cave.

Sounds a lot like today right? So many pastors and too few shepherds that smell like, their own sheep. John C Maxwell wrote a good example of this in "Leadership Promises for Every Day: A Daily Devotional."

"There are leaders that attract followers and leaders that attract other leaders!"

David was that man.

David left Gath and escaped to the cave of Adullam. When his brothers and his father heard about it –All those that were in distress or in debt or discontented gathered around him; and he became their leader! About 400 men were with him.

From there David went to Mizpah in Moab and said to the king of Moab "Would you let my father and mother come and stay with you UNTIL I LEARN what God will do for me? So he left them with the king of Moab and they stayed as long as David was in the stronghold. But the prophet Gad said to David "Do not stay in the stronghold. Go into the land of Judah." So David left and went to the forest of Hereth. 1 Samuel 22:1-5 (New International Version)

This is beautiful when God promises to take you out of the stronghold, especially when you get yourself out of something only to find yourself right back in a cave.

I think that if this was in our era for David he would have taken a selfie in the Cave of Adullum. How else would they hear about him there? He checked himself in at the cave of Adullum much like many of us do with the ER hospital wrist bands as "my current status" on Facebook, Instagram and Snapchat. But in our life there are always going to be real followers and God will send you real friends to you when you need it the most. Not the ones that are not present or willing to help in times of distress. Real friends are with you in distress and throughout your stress.

David was basically saying to his men, "I don't know right

now – it looks bleak at the moment. I have NO clue or ANY idea what to do – except fight! Can you do that with me?"

They were there.

> *I cry aloud to the Lord; I lift up my voice to the Lord for mercy. I pour out before him my complaint; before him I tell my trouble.*
>
> *When my spirit grows faint within me, it is you who watch over my way. In the path where I walk people have hidden a snare for me. Look and see, there is no one at my right hand; no one is concerned for me. I have no refuge; no one cares for my life.* Psalm 142 (New International Version)

David also appears to be bipolar. He suffered with severe stages of depression. He was a man with a heavy state and case of the blues in his life. His moods varied and they were recorded for our learning. David was a journalist –a person who collects/gathers, writes or distributes news or other current information. He was openly declaring and writing his case to God and this became the Word distributed to the world!

Many individuals suffer from some form of depression. There is healing.

In Psalm 56:1-9 David cries out again–

Be merciful to me, O God, for man would swallow me up;

What Cave Are You In

Fighting all day he oppresses me.
My enemies would hound *me* all day,
For *there are* many who fight against me, O Most High.

Whenever I am afraid,
I will trust in You.
In God (I will praise His word),
In God I have put my trust;
I will not fear.
What can flesh do to me?

All day they twist my words;
All their thoughts *are* against me for evil.
They gather together,
They hide, they mark my steps,
When they lie in wait for my life.
Shall they escape by iniquity?
In anger cast down the peoples, O God!

You number my wanderings;
Put my tears into Your bottle;
Are they not in Your book?
When I cry out *to You,*
Then my enemies will turn back;
This I know, because God *is* for me.

Not only did David have to conquer depression, he also had to conquer fear and he had to conquer brokenness.

Just because he was a skilled fighter doesn't mean that never made him afraid. He had to battle with that as well. Often times this left him in a lowly state. David was broken many times in his life. Being broken is not a defeat! It is an admission. It is your building block. In your brokenness you will find your breakthrough. Being broken doesn't mean that you don't work; it means that you are not functioning PROPERLY and this is exactly where God moves in to do the rest of the work when you surrender your life to Him.

Being under a constant attack is also not defeat! It is not because you are weak! It is because you are strong, because you are a fighter and a warrior. Strong walls shake but don't collapse. Whatever life throws at us, even if it hurts, we have to be strong through God and fight through it. Sometimes in these cases our lives have to be completely shaken up, changed and rearranged to bring us to the place we are meant to be. There are walls that need to be torn down in order to be REBUILT!

We have to stand strong. We have to find a place that when all else is fallen, we stand up in Christ! Do what you can and God will do what YOU CAN'T!

Remember every flower must grow through dirt. Unfortunately, in life there is a lot of dirt but it makes us blossom and grow. Our roots become developed this way. We grow strong roots in Christ.

I reflected on this quote even when I came back from that life impacting, life empowering, life altering and life changing retreat that says:

> **Perhaps the butterfly is proof that you can go through a great deal of darkness yet become something…BEAUTIFUL.**

Just put your trust in GOD!!! Behind those smiles from a painful life is hidden strength. But when you give that to God to uncover all that, He will build you up again – better than ever!

A brand *new you* and a better you! Isn't that what you want? Let truth be your shield and buckler (Psalm 91). What's done is done. It is what it is. Get over it and move on already and allow that brokenness and the story behind you be your victory. Be free of all of that – the word of God will always prevail as it states THE TRUTH SHALL SET YOU FREE!

People are walking around with the "blessed and highly favored" face on – that's the real mask. If something's wrong – say it! State that! That is what intercession is for and a true lamenting for change. Give to God a full surrendered life and submission. That is not always easy. It is VERY difficult!

You will always have to battle with two wars. As for me, I am constantly waging war and it changes day by day. Whether it is the absence of something, feeling a certain way, battling emotions, battling my past, thoughts, memories, dreams, doubt, fear, pain, discouragement, anger, frustration or anything that tries to creep up and pull me away from a focused place with God. It will always creep up, but there is a way.

Jesus was distinct – the outspoken. The one that didn't fit in, because he was born to stand out! We discover our purpose during these times. We come out of the cave and pull others with us. We can't save the multitudes, Jesus did all that. But we help. We CAN make disciples – that is really the command.

You may be wondering, why is this attack so constant for you. You may even be scaring people sometimes –family, friends –or anyone near you. Be careful, because sometimes in your attack, you can end up attacking and hurting others. You are not the only one under attack. Sometimes that defensive wall is the first that God needs to break to take you out of that mess.

So let it be mental, physical, emotional or spiritual! We are all at WAR saints!!! It is not just you. We are being attacked in dreams and from the moment we wake up. There are attacks at the job. Home is on the horizon, as we are working diligently to have a balance. We even try to uplift others when we need the uplifting too, but that is life. An ongoing cycle.

"When you admit your weakness you place yourself in the strongest position possible!" Serenity Bible NKJV, A Companion for 12 Step Recovery

In the hands of GOD! You will find yourself weak in MANY areas! The difference is knowing that and recognizing immediately where God needs to come in! He is the one that will validate us!

> ***Through God we will do valiantly for it is HE who shall tread down our enemies.*** Psalm 60:12 (New King James Version)

The refuge in a cave cannot save David. God alone can

bring his soul out of prison as he cried out!

> ***Set me free from my prison, that I may praise your name. Then the righteous will gather about me because of your goodness to me.*** Psalm 142: 7 (New International Version)

Remember lamentation is necessary and a lot of times we don't even want to go there to fully surrender our broken lives to God. Full! ALL! Everything!!!! Let it out – Let it go – Pour out! This is all part of recovery.

This is where grieving begins – cleanses us on the inside and cleanses our wounds so the healing can begin. It hurts but He cleanses us. It hurts but He empties us so we can be filled with what God has for us which is far greater and far better than any other thing we try to hold on to.

We give up in order to win! What looks like a no-win situation to us is actually a win-win situation to God.

Let go of the past, let go of the situation! Easier said than done – yes but we need to obliterate the history that keeps causing the mystery. We need God to take us from this caved way of thinking! You know how hard it is for us. Every day we will struggle to go back to the place where we felt like the world was the best. But God says no. God says enough. God says don't go there. God says don't go back! And as much as we pout, cry, kick, scream, yell, frustrate, resist… We are being emptied of everything so that God can fill us with all the good that He has for us!

Whatever cave that you find yourself in, when you feel like

EVERYTHING is going wrong –inside AND out. It becomes the perfect place for God to show you and teach you that you won't be moved by it. It is not going to move you. Get used to the storms and battles of life because they are used as the fuel to push through. You have learned the secret! You have learned the secret—to be content in all things. When you have no other choice you make a commitment.

Commitment is an act of committing, pledging or engaging oneself. A pledge, promise, obligation, involvement; to give in trust – pledge oneself, entrust – to do or deliver for treatment "surrender a complete life".

I can no longer go where I want to go. I can no longer have what I want to have. I can no longer say what I want to say. I have to go where God tells me and have what He has for me. It is not about me. It is about the promise.

It is a stage of constant growing. You have to practice what you preach. You have to be that example for real, even if you fall, get up, get over it and move on again and again and again. God is your source!

There is an army rising up that will be formed! David was forming an army here starting in the cave. Don't just spend time with others, invest time in others. Deposit in them to do… reproduce yourself.

> Leaders add infinite weight to their words by reincarnating the principles they teach. Paul never asked the Corinthian church to do something he never did. His leadership was on display and open

for ridicule, willing to play the fool in order to model the surrendered life. Endured mocking from others, didn't waiver, sacrificed luxuries others enjoyed, urged his followers to imitate his life. God's kingdom is not about talk but about POWER! John C. Maxwell, Leadership Promises for Every Day: A Daily Devotional.

Remember at the end of the day there will always be some battle to face, some ongoing war – and the one you will have to confront first and foremost is YOU!

Demonstrate strength character, humility, grace, love commitment, truth, virtue, and stance – GET BACK UP! Be free in the truth of God's Word.

In order to be renewed we cannot keep being a prisoner of our past. We HAVE to let go. WE must let go of all the things that are tearing us apart. Get out of that cave. What is your prison cell?

Maybe it's a relationship.

Maybe it's a workplace.

Maybe it's a health issue.

Maybe it's your finances.

Maybe it's your living conditions.

Maybe it's your own attitude.

Maybe it's your mind.

Maybe it's an issue with people.

Maybe it's social media.

Or maybe you are in the same situation as the Apostle Paul with real confinement by incarceration. Whatever the situation is, MINISTER THERE! Be a vessel there. Many moments you will have to speak victory over your own life! The choir is not coming home with you, the sermon is over, friends go home and people move on. Now what? We make everything such a huge issue when it is not really going to help you by frustrating your soul.

The prison should never limit you!

Nothing can limit the work of God!

We can remain stuck being a prisoner of our past! We never move forward. We just stay stagnant over past relationships, past abuse, past pain or any type of uncomfortable experience. We fail to progress. Trauma can trap you based on your perception.

We can't remain there! Remember, God promises to restore all that we lost! God promises to heal the brokenhearted. God promises…but we want to remain in our own type of prison. Why?

What are you so fixated on?

What is the stronghold?

Why is the wall still up?

What has you confined?

The same way David was freed from that cave so can we be. Joseph was freed from his prison cell. The three Hebrew boys were freed from the furnace.

To be confined is to be limited or restricted or unable to leave a place because of illness, imprisonment, etc. Sometimes we are not able to leave a "place" that we have built up in our minds or because of our situations. We become limited and restricted.

LET IT GO!

BE FREE!

You know I had come to imagine Paul in that prison cell. Dirty, hungry, scrawny, sitting on a concrete surface and using this opportunity to encourage himself and the church. In your place of the worst–what do you find yourself doing? Discouraging or encouraging? Stressing or stretching your faith? Isolating or coming out from the dark into the light?

> *Now I want you to know, brothers and sisters, that what has happened to me has actually served to advance the gospel. As a result, it has become clear throughout the whole palace guard and to everyone else that I am in chains for Christ. And because of my chains, most of the brothers and sisters have become confident in the Lord and dare all the more to proclaim the gospel without fear.* Philippians 1:12-14 (New International Version)

In all of this Paul learned the secret to keep his peace

despite the circumstance. In every situation there was a way for him to still excel and advance no matter where he found himself.

> ***Whatever you have learned or received or heard from me, or seen in me—put it into practice. And the God of peace will be with you.*** Philippians 4:9 (New International Version)

> ***I know what it is to be in need, and I know what it is to have plenty. I have learned the secret of being content in any and every situation, whether well fed or hungry, whether living in plenty or in want.*** Philippians 4:12 (New International Version)

We just need to leave it in the hands of God. During all testing and trials, keep the faith and keep speaking life. Speak life to others…Maybe your situation is extremely difficult, but being in a prison for real is difficult, yet they manage a way. They find hope. They find peace. They find joy. They release from all and that is through God. That is the best ministering, when you know what it is like to pull through when you have had some "chains" in your life.

In this place we will give this up in a prayer…

"Dear Lord,

We are going to vet this out together. I don't care how long it takes at this point, for I am not sure. I have been asking, questioning and pondering all of these things. But I recognize that I can no longer be confined because of my pain or problems. Break me out of a prison mentality. I have reached the end of my rope and have reached a point of no return. What cannot be is the reality and so is the pain that accompanies that truth. There is a point where we say – SO BE IT! LET IT BE! It is what it is and I am now letting go–because I am thinking this is how. In my mind, I clearly see what is left for me to do…nothing but let it all out and all go until this has been removed from me. Help me in this. I know that You are not going anywhere and that You are not going to leave my side. Help me cope each day in a new life, for you are my coping mechanism. You are my shoulder to lean on. You are my arm and strength. You are the One who will hold me up when I feel none. Every tear shed is one You know all too well and are familiar with all my grief–I am not afraid. When things try to surface, I will keep releasing it all and hold on to none of it. Remove me from this slaved way of living mentally, physically and spiritually. This is it! There is a new found hope in You. I want to know You more and I want to grow. I know that in all that I have experienced, my "chains" will advance the gospel and establish a true purpose. In every situation that I find myself—a pit, a ditch, a cave or prison You keep me safe and rescue me. I thank You Lord for keeping me through it all."

Amen

REBUILT: Beginning the Ending

PIECE 7

DESTROY IT

Some things in your life were sent your way that you think are a blessing but are actually sent to destroy you! My advice – be wise, is it really good? [Philippians 4:8]

So before this takes you out slowly but surely and completely...

DESTROY WHAT DESTROYS YOU!!!!!

The devil is angry but he cannot win!!! And he is going to stop at nothing to take you out! The reason why you have been so persecuted is because he knows his time is **short!** He's pulling out all the stops and trying to pull us down in every way that he can.

> *"Therefore rejoice, O heavens, and you who dwell in them! Woe to the inhabitants of the earth and the sea! For the devil has come down to you, having great wrath, because he knows that he has a short time."* Now when

the dragon saw that he had been cast to the earth, he persecuted the woman who gave birth to the male Child. But the woman was given two wings of a great eagle, that she might fly into the wilderness to her place, where she is nourished for a time and times and half a time, from the presence of the serpent. So the serpent spewed water out of his mouth like a flood after the woman, that he might cause her to be carried away by the flood. But the earth helped the woman, and the earth opened its mouth and swallowed up the flood which the dragon had spewed out of his mouth. And the dragon was enraged with the woman, and he went to make war with the rest of her offspring, who keep the commandments of God and have the testimony of Jesus Christ." Revelations 12:12-17 (New King James Version)

You have been experiencing challenges. The minute you came to the Savior for renewal and recovery, the attack became more fierce. Everywhere!!! In the scriptures you will find "The Why" behind those challenges and "The Why" you have the victory.

No weapon *formed against you shall prosper, And every tongue which rises against you in judgment You shall condemn. This is the heritage of the servants of the Lord, And their righteousness is from Me," Says the Lord.* Isaiah 54:17 (New King James Version)

It is a lying spirit that has been attacking you. He shows us

Destroy It

in dreams and we attack it in prayer. The devil uses people close to us...he is an EXPERT at manipulating Christians. But we have to gear up and know that our war is not against flesh and blood [Ephesians 6]. Attack it in the spirit realm through prayer!!!

The fight is in the spirit. He wants you to see exactly what to attack. Jealousy, envy and every other ill thing that brings frustration. For us, our ministry is a deliverance ministry. It is about snatching people out of the grip of demons. He attacks our ministry and body. But we gear up!

Do a "pre-attack" in an offensive position.
Be on guard, be ready.
We take authority.

Lying spirits and accusing spirits say, "You're a failure, worthless, unattractive, incapable, you don't measure up or that you are never going to make it!" Those are lying spirits. Don't respond to what you are not! Respond to what YOU ARE! Say, "That's not my name I don't respond to that."

Just because you failed doesn't mean you are a failure.
Just because you lost doesn't mean you are a loser.

Jesus wrote us a prescription labeled "BIBLE." Keep believing and you will see the fruit rise up. People will see with their own eyes what the Lord says. The ones putting you down are the ones that wish to take your place.

He wants you to destroy yourself. That's why he loves suicide! Wow!

But have NO fear…God says, "My grace is sufficient for thee [2 Corinthians 12:9]."

The serpent was subtler than any other beast. When she ate the fruit she died spiritually. She was separated from God [Genesis 3:1].

We eat the fruit. We believe the lie.

Many times we have gone out of our way to get out of God's way. Meaning we would be so up to our noses with addictions, struggles, problems and sin that we could never find our own way back. We would have to be rescued by the One who had the only ability to do so.

But for choosing the "all in or nothing" lifestyle we would hit rock bottom every single time when we were headed in one direction! Because that direction would lead down to death.

I have heard so many times from others, "In life we will only have moments, so that's what we live for!"

WRONG again!!!

That mindset becomes the 'One Direction' of behavior and that is extremely destructive. This is a place where we don't know our limits. We roll that dice going all in or nothing and never count the costs or consequences of our actions. We think, "Oh well I already thought it, been there, done that and I got this far—so I might as well do it all!" It becomes wild and wasteful living. Irresponsible and unconcerned behavior rises as we continue to drown out the voice of God and our mentors.

Destroy It

The bible says not to call one "a fool" but darn it — I was the BIGGEST FOOL of all! Just stuck on stupid! Seriously! I am not even kidding. I could tell you in all honesty I never knew my limits. I was the wayward woman. The one back on serious dosages of alcohol. I was the one causing havoc to no end.

We certainly have gone to extremes to head down to the worst pathway. Why did we go out of our way to do it?

REMEMBER ROCK BOTTOM!

And how you met the ROCK (Jesus) at that bottom!

His value in your life means more than any trick, trip or try! You got this!!! He is more than any man or woman on this earth. He is more than any job. More than any place! God truly is it! He is the Maker and Master of all things! This is another opportunity to do things RIGHT! Now it is time to go ALL in and out of our way FOR GOD. We will rise above our enemies.

My pastor shared with us, "How long will you allow the devil to walk around in your mind with his dirty, stinky feet?"

We can stop him because just like that– he is after us in that one direction. He typically comes at us with the same old things, with the same temptations and with the same stricks thrown our way to try and trip us up.

He knew you would take that swig!
He knew you would take that hit!

He knew you would take that deal!
He knew you would take that steal!
He knew you would just give in!
He knows your weakness and places that make you stumble!!!

But I am declaring over my life and those of others, that we have entered an abundantly blessed season. This is the season of blessing! This is where God is on the scene because we are saying YES! Because we are following HIM! Because we are doing what's right!!! So keep doing what you are doing and don't allow that dirty, stinky and rotten devil any room to trip you up!!!

Arguments!
Addictions!
Anger!
Anguish!

> ***The Lord will grant that the enemies who rise up against you will be defeated before you. They will come at you from one direction but flee from you in seven.*** Deuteronomy 28:7 (New International Version)

The enemy comes in ONE DIRECTION! ONE WAY! He is not that good! We give him way too much credit! God is stronger! You are stronger! You are wiser than your enemies!!!! Don't allow the enemy to keep trampling his dirty little feet all over your territory. You belong to God and can walk in His ways!

Keep that in your mind that he hasn't changed his strategy. He is still trying to deceive the same way. That is the reason he is doing that. Once you believe in your mind that's what you become. Don't believe the lies of the devil. He's a liar! He hates you because you look just like God. He hates you because you are a worshiper and you took his role.

Proverbs 23:7 says, "As a man thinks in his heart so is he."

So you look like Papa! Once you know who you are in Christ you will never answer to a lie again!

> ***"We are hard-pressed on every side, yet not crushed; we are perplexed, but not in despair; persecuted, but not forsaken; struck down, but not destroyed— always carrying about in the body the dying of the Lord Jesus, that the life of Jesus also may be manifested in our body."*** 2 Corinthians 4:8-10

> ***"They that keep their minds stayed on you will be kept in perfect peace."*** Isaiah 26:3

Speak what you want to have and what you want to obtain. Give it to God. God is able and He is faithful. He is not a man that He shall lie. If He made a promise, it will come to pass! If you stay faithful. If you get out of the will of God, then you get out of position to receive it. You will be filled with doubt, uncertainty or confusion and remain perplexed!

Sometimes things happen and we don't understand why- repeat "My grace is sufficient for you!"

You have an enemy and he has not hung up his boxing gloves. Come with the word every time.

No matter the situation or the sickness. Speak the word EVERY time!!!

In the beginning was the word and the word was God [John 1].

Cast down but not destroyed. Persecuted but not destroyed. Rejection can come in many forms and many times in your life. At some point everyone has experienced this. People who are hurt, hurt other people. Hurting people need healing. Time doesn't heal all wounds! God does! Jesus heals ALL WOUNDS! The time is to get you to adjust to a new manner of living.

There was a woman in the bible by the name of Hannah in 1 Samuel 1:5. She was tormented by her enemy and her condition. She was vexed in her soul.

Is there something that you are believing for that you have not seen the manifestation of? That is causing you to be vexed? Put action behind your faith. Do something to show God– I believe and I receive!

The Lord remembered Hannah and gave her more children. My God has supplied all my needs [Philippians 4:19]. You have to shut the voice of PENINNAH! Make the tables turn.

God has given your own song of victory. Yes, He has already.

Destroy anything that tries to destroy you!

PIECE 8
WHEN BEAUTY IS TOXIC

Wikipedia states that the *Amanita Muscaria* is a mushroom that is beautiful to behold but can be very toxic. Not fatal but it can cause sickness. A lot of things in life we note as beautiful yet they can be **dangerous** and actually cause sickness. What about the things that we want that are beautiful but that are not for us?

I woke one morning and immediately read Proverbs 31. This is the passage on the virtuous woman. What is a virtuous [conforming to moral and ethical principles; morally excellent; upright] woman? What does she possess? What gives her virtue, an effective force, an influence or power?

The Virtuous Wife

Who can find a virtuous wife?
For her worth is far above rubies.
The heart of her husband safely trusts her;

REBUILT: Beginning the Ending

So he will have no lack of gain.
She does him good and not evil
All the days of her life.
She seeks wool and flax,
And willingly works with her hands.
She is like the merchant ships,
She brings her food from afar.
She also rises while it is yet night,
And provides food for her household,
And a portion for her maidservants.
She considers a field and buys it;
From her profits she plants a vineyard.
She girds herself with strength,
And strengthens her arms.
She perceives that her merchandise is good,
And her lamp does not go out by night.
She stretches out her hands to the distaff,
And her hand holds the spindle.
She extends her hand to the poor,
Yes, she reaches out her hands to the needy.
She is not afraid of snow for her household,
For all her household is clothed with scarlet.
She makes tapestry for herself;
Her clothing is fine linen and purple.
Her husband is known in the gates,
When he sits among the elders of the land.
She makes linen garments and sells them,
And supplies sashes for the merchants.
Strength and honor are her clothing;
She shall rejoice in time to come.
She opens her mouth with wisdom,

And on her tongue is the law of kindness.
She watches over the ways of her household,
And does not eat the bread of idleness.
Her children rise up and call her blessed;
Her husband also, and he praises her:
"Many daughters have done well,
But you excel them all."
Charm is deceitful and beauty is passing,
But a woman who fears the Lord, she shall be praised.
Give her of the fruit of her hands,
And let her own works praise her in the gates.
Proverbs 31:10-31 (New King James Version)

This sounds like the most amazing woman in the world. She has it all together. She is noted for all her good deeds. But I just love how the scripture closes because it explains the most exceptional detail about her that gives her virtue–she fears the Lord. She has reverence for God, a respect for God, a recognition for God that is first and foremost.

> **Charm is deceitful and beauty is passing, But a woman who fears the Lord, She shall be praised.**

It is not about the deeds that make you beautiful. It is not what you do on the outward appearance that make you beautiful. It is not even things that you have or acquire that make you beautiful. For all the natural things will eventually fade away. But it is the inside that matters most of all. It is having an ever-lasting relationship with the Father that makes you beautiful. This changes your look. This makes you glow. This makes you radiate.

Everything else is just passing. Things last from moment to moment. Sometimes we even beg for the most beautiful things that we see. We look at something and we call it BEAUTIFUL.

A beautiful person.
A beautiful figure.
A beautiful home.
A beautiful car.
A beautiful bag.
A beautiful dress.
A beautiful pair of shoes.... etc.

Things attractive to the eyes. This is what we look for and what we gravitate to. But what about when those things that fade away or when they are not as beautiful as you think. You notice someone and think they are the most beautiful person in the world based on that outward appearance.

> *"But the Lord said to Samuel, "Do not look at his appearance or at his physical stature, because I have refused him. For the Lord does not see as man sees; for man looks at the outward appearance, but the Lord looks at the heart."* 1 Samuel 16:7 (New King James Version)

Meanwhile, they have bad intentions, they lie, they hurt people, they do the wrong things... that is not quite so beautiful anymore! That is what you call toxic! Just like the mushroom. It looks so beautiful, colorful and attractive but it can get you sick inside. Why then even go near it? Why should you become enticed by something that will eventually make you sick? It is simply not worth it. Leave behind the 5 inch beauties in those heels because after 5 minutes of usage they will give you some serious blisters! Again, it is just not worth it. A cupcake is delicious but it is the kale that is nutritious.

In the book of Genesis, Eve was in the Garden of Eden with her mate. She had all that she needed. But then she came to a point to "want". It was only until the serpent deceived her that she came to think that she needed the fruit too. The fruit became a want…and so the want became her need…until her eyes were opened and she tasted her way to the place of death. The serpent talked her so much into believing the lie–that she will not die if she ate the fruit. The truth was–she didn't die immediately but she took the ultimate eternal plan that God had and brought death to humankind.

We have to be so careful in this life. You may have such a desire for a thing but just leave it. Ask God to help you and to stir up healthy desires. All this can be controlled when you bring it to the place where it belongs. Under the subjection of God. He will give us what we need. Everywhere I turned I can see God shouting from the rooftops… "I know what you *want*…but I am giving you what you *need*."

He will give you the most beautiful things. We just need to be reverent before Him. We need to have that relationship with Him and ask when beauty will be toxic for us. The warning signs will emerge.

All things *are lawful for me, but* ***not all things*** *are helpful;*

> ***All things*** *are lawful for me, but **not all things edify**.*
> 1 Corinthians 10:23 (New King James Version)

God help us! Protect us from the things that cause us to be sick inside. And if something has made us sick – take it out! All of it! Remove anything that is not good for us. Bring us to the place of complete health and wholeness so that we can glorify Your name in all that we do.

We could be that virtuous woman that God is trying to build or the one that is perishing. That is the old self that needed to die. She was so beautiful. She was sexy. She was passionate. She was exciting. She was so trendy and fashionable. She was popular. She was successful. She was talented. She would work all through her days. She was wild. She was crazy. She loved to party and have a good time. She could have any man. She had no rules, no restrictions and no limits. No one could tell her anything…because she was just unstoppable in all her ways. She wanted to hide the pain. Only one thing she didn't realize.

She was perishing!

Sometimes she is missed. The old self. The one that was dying. But God knew what He was doing when He saved her. So she came to her senses and realized that too. Thank God He saved her!

> **"In that while we were still sinners, Christ died for the ungodly."** Romans 5:6 (New King James Version)

No matter what boat we find ourselves in, there will always

come the day that we cry out, "LORD SAVE US!" We find ourselves in a situation that we uniquely created. Beautifully stationed for us. To carry us through–OUR WAY! We drive! We go! We move! According to how we feel is best for us. Just living from moment to moment.

You think this is what God desires for us? A stormy and crazy life? A big mess with no restrictions? No saving for us…and headed towards death row? Not quite! God is our Savior! He came to save and deliver us. Whatever road we take, God is already in it waiting for us to come to our senses and call out to Him! It is so funny how we think we have it all together. Eventually the cares of this world will have its weight and price. The excitement ceases and reality bites. Make way for the crash and burn.

WAIT! There is still time!

> *What a wretched man I am! Who will rescue me from this body that is subject to death? Thanks be to God, who delivers me through Jesus Christ our Lord!*
> Romans 7:24-25 (New International Version)

You can call out to Jesus! Ask Him to save you and He will. You can invite Him in your heart. He has always been following you throughout your journey. He can see you. He is resting and waiting for you. When you cry out–there He will always be! Rest assured, that is the God that we serve. He is our hero! He is the One to pull us out of the water when we are drowning. He is the One to calm the storm. He is the One to begin that change in us. He is the One to remove the habit. He is the One to die down the addiction. He is the One that will make you beautiful inside. He is the one that will be your husband. He is the One that will give you good success in all that you do.

> *Be strong and of good courage, for to this people you shall divide as an inheritance the land which I swore to their fathers to give them. Only be strong and very courageous, that you may observe to do according to all the law which Moses My servant commanded you; do not turn from it to the right hand or to the left, that you may prosper wherever you go. This Book of the Law shall not depart from your mouth, but you shall meditate in it day and night, that you may observe to do according to all that is written in it. For then you will make your way prosperous, and then you will have good success.* Joshua 1:6-8 (New King James Version)

Whatever situation you are in. Whatever road you decide to take. Whatever journey you wish to walk, find the one that brings you good success. Don't allow yourself to be dazzled by the toxic things in life just by sight. For all the things of the world will never give you an everlasting joy and freedom the way the choices do with God. He doesn't want you to perish. He doesn't want you to drown. He doesn't want you to lose control. He doesn't want you to hurt anymore.

God wants you to have a good life. He wants you to trust in Him. He wants you to depend on Him as your source that never runs dry. He wants you to give Him access to every area in your life.

> *For this reason I bow my knees to the Father of our Lord*

When Beauty Is Toxic

Jesus Christ, from whom the whole family in heaven and earth is named, that He would grant you, according to the riches of His glory, to be strengthened with might through His Spirit in the inner man, that Christ may dwell in your hearts through faith; that you, being rooted and grounded in love, may be able to comprehend with all the saints what is the width and length and depth and height— to know the love of Christ which passes knowledge; that you may be filled with all the fullness of God. Now to Him who is able to do exceedingly abundantly above all that we ask or think, according to the power that works in us, to Him be glory in the church by Christ Jesus to all generations, forever and ever. Amen. Ephesians 3:14-21 (New King James Version)

You don't have to perish from toxic sources. You can have a good life! Cry out and He will save you from perishing!

That is the beginning of your ending. When you die to self you become alive in Him. This is a huge part of being renewed, restored and rebuilt.

Some of the most beautiful things in life are easily found in all the wrong places. But the darkest things and hidden places and things that take so long to surface—those become more beautiful than anything else. That is what He has been prompting to develop in us.

My prayer is that the words found in this book would catapult you into the arms of our Savior so that your journey for complete healing can serve its purpose. Amen.

REBUILT: Beginning the Ending

PIECE 9
NO MORE RELAPSE

"Emotions are temporary so don't let them permanently destroy you!" – Jessenia Munoz

I responded, "Thank you for sharing and being led by the Spirit to encourage others experiencing an emotional mess!" For I would have to say that would be me most days. When I wake up missing a thing and feeling a huge void in my soul. It makes me sad. I went to see if "miss" was an emotion and it kind of is because it means "absence, loss & want". For me that runs deep when I have to give up the things I miss the most! I feel the absence of that every day and it hurts! It hurts me a lot. I try to remind myself of all the good things but that one little thing can sometimes be so impactful that it can put a dent in me and I can feel it. My emotions go off the wall and then I find myself in a place where I think I am weak again. It was good to read that blog written by Jessenia Munoz because that lets me know that God wants to use all that He can to remind me of my

promise and not the **problem**. Everything around me seems contrary to that promise but I know I have to press forward - reach forward and look ahead to all that God has for me. It is getting past pain that is the hardest part for me and that takes time, too much of it. For day to day that can vary depending on the situation. I pray that God seals up every hole, every crack, every crevice and every area that is in WANT or that feels a loss. King David with all his wives, concubines, children, money, status, houses and more felt such an absence. There had to be a "one little thing" for him too. He said **"The Lord is my Shepherd, I shall not be in want"** Psalm 23.

I have to put these fluctuating feelings in God's hands and pray for the spirit of Joy to OVERTAKE ME EVERYDAY so that I won't feel an absence anymore! God help me!!! For I know that all the mighty men in the bible suffered in their weakest moments. Apostle Paul wrote "Rejoice always, and again I say rejoice" in Philippians 4:4 while being in a prison cell. Sometimes I find myself in the prison cell of my mind and I want an escape! I don't want to be held captive any more by my emotions! No more!

Relapse! Now what?

1. To fall or slip back into a former state, practice, etc.: "to relapse into silence."

2. To fall back into illness after convalescence [gradual recovery of health and strength after illness] or apparent recovery.

3. To fall back into vice, wrongdoing, or error; backslide:

I try to encourage myself a lot. Also encourage others – smile, talk, help, hug and be there when I realize I can't even do all that well. I fall short in that too. I can't be at every place at one time. That is why I write too, so that these words can travel.

The truth is – I miss what I lost. I miss it a whole lot. I miss my own stubborn life at times. And as the days pass – I miss it more. I want to forget and lose myself in anything that will dilute the pain. Those are the days I have to press through stronger.

It is as horrible as losing my best friend and now there is no more refuge. Every place I turn, it is nowhere and that hurts me so much. Like I'm having such a hard time coping and dealing with this process.

I feel myself slipping every day. I want something to make sense and FEEL RIGHT. I'm slipping.

Before I went to the retreat I wrote the following on a post-it and pinned it to my journal page:

> Step 2 "Came to believe that a power greater than ourselves could restore us to sanity."
> Serenity Bible, A Companion for 12 Step Recovery
>
> We can't fix ourselves or do anything on our own.
>
> Embed yourself in the Word of God!

I always have to hide my tears. *Addiction* is the state of being enslaved to a habit or practice to something that is psychologically or physically habit forming, as narcotics, to such an extent that its cessation [temporary or complete stopping] causing severe trauma [an experience that produces psychological injury or pain]. *Pain* is a distressing emotion, mental or emotional suffering or torment.

It takes time – to reconstruct and readjust your attitude of life, God, yourself & your surroundings but never give up! **RECOVERY IS POSSIBLE!**

I need time and a lot of it. Sometimes to be alone, to think, heal, process, reflect and readjust before I try coming up for air. This is my peace. This is my haven…everyone is gone and I am in a tranquil environment. I pray, I read, I write. I love this time, especially when my mind has shut down so much. It's like I don't even want to talk sometimes or out loud, because obviously I'm still thinking, processing and analyzing mentally, so I write. I write it here. It's personal, it's private, and it gets out. That is my release. I don't care for crowds when I feel nonfunctional. I need to pray and regroup until I am functional.

When I am ready I get back out. Then I am better. I need that time to deal with me too. That's difficult and I am not afraid to admit that I am a difficult one.

A friend told me "don't let anyone tell you or make you do what you don't want to do. Don't go where you don't want to go."

Friday prayer meet came and I stood home this time. My mind was bombarded. I didn't feel like I was appropriate or well for any interaction. I need a revitalizing life source experience that is so thick, rich, and powerful to shake all this off me, my mind, my heart, my soul. So impactful to supersede all else, to drown everything away. How could this be because the human part is the weakest! Like I do need the presence of God radiating, filling and taking over in my life so these natural tears can go away. It is so easy for me to cry and feel the pain and feel everything that I'm missing and I can't function this way. My life has become unmanageable. I need to be restored to sanity, a new sanity. A sound and healthy place because this is right now. My mind like this – is not healthy. So where's the step about renewing the mind forever. I need that because I struggle to shake these things off my head.

I'm afraid.

> *"Do not be afraid for I have ransomed you. I have called you by name; you are mine.* **WHEN** *you go through deep waters, I will be with you.* **WHEN** *you go through rivers of difficulty, you will not drown.* **WHEN** *you walk through the fire of oppression, you will not be burned up; the flames will not consume you. For I am the Lord, your God."* Isaiah 43:1-3

I like to define words so that I can somehow understand better exactly what is happening to me.

You see the thing is that sometimes as I write it with the impression to help others in mind and it brings a balm of healing to my own life! Writing in general just helps me a lot to cope and deal with life. I love to write. Just don't realize how sometimes things can get so severe.

Honestly I don't think I can even explain the severity or the depth of my situation to anyone. These are the pages that really just go between me and God.

The truth is I am in this process because I suffered profusely with deep cases of depression. When I am trying to let go, it is making me miserable. I need something in the interim to lift off the misery and quite frankly that has not settled or eased the pain just yet.

I have those moments where I am overanalyzing everything. I look at other people's happy pictures and I'm like, "Wow…I wish I had that just alone." I can't express any greater than this that I have never felt this sad in all my life without the one thing I felt I needed in my life. I am experiencing the slowest death in the world. I think the old Christina didn't die…she is dying. And that hurts. There is no resurrecting her. The bible says hope deferred makes the heart sick and the old Christina has hopes and dreams still. And who can I share that with?

How do you tell your family, your friends or anyone the true source of your pain? How to you explain the unexplainable? What is worse is when you have to finish all this because you started it. And all that was done in secret now you feel yourself suffer in secret. Yet, the pain of all this is so present, so loud and so demanding. Never has anything hurt me like this. Having to put this all behind me is almost impossible. I say almost because I know there has got to be a better way when I surrendered my will…it's just being in a miserable place that I did all of this and that is not fair.

I constantly feel that pressing upon me that I can't talk to anyone one. I can't explain to anyone. I am forcing myself to eat, talk, smile, function, and dress even though I look like a mess. I have never been so sad. And this sadness is a sin.

That is the battle with depression. When you are not well at all. I know this all isn't true. The enemy plays all these things on rewind. Now we have to cut the tape from playing and move forward.

My counselor advised me that I was prone to relapse. That moments like this would occur but I have to fight through this. I know I am being stretched in every area. It hurts but I know it is good for me. I am going to stretch out to others when I feel myself failing. I know I can't do this alone. There is support. There is an answer for me. I never had to face this alone—I chose that and when I did I wallowed in that way too long. Precise plan of Satan!

I don't want to relapse. I am not going to fear this.

Not sure if I am the only one that feels this way. One day I feel like that tree that has no leaves, completely bare and stripped. Other days I feel like that oak tree so planted and filled with beautiful and colorful leaves. In every case to God, I believe we still light up before Him.

So I am guessing that is how Peter felt when he denied Jesus 3 times and then on the day of Pentecost when he stood up and 3 thousand were added that day! What a way to bounce back!

Peter fell forward! God is good.

It is just getting through those bare days, keeping in focus and in alignment with the purpose of God over your life. Jesus help us to get through it! I keep hearing you loud in my soul so I know that you are close by during these times that seem to vary over my life. It is not like I am here standing alone. It just looks that way at times. It's just a moment then I know You are pressing upon me that mandate. I am here for that.

> ***Now Peter was sitting out in the courtyard, and a servant girl came to him. "You also were with Jesus of Galilee," she said. But he denied it before them all. "I don't know what you're talking about," he said. Then he went out to the gateway, where another servant girl saw him and said to the people there, "This fellow was with Jesus of Nazareth." He denied it again, with an oath: "I don't know the man!" After a little while, those standing there went up to Peter and said, "Surely you are one of them; your accent gives you away." Then he began to call down curses, and he swore to them, "I don't know the man!" Immediately a rooster crowed. Then Peter remembered the word Jesus had spoken: "Before the rooster crows, you will disown me three times." And he went outside and wept bitterly.*** Matthew 26:69-75 (New King James Version)

This is a good place to be because when we were bad, we would be so careless, "Oh well!" Then continue down the pathway of death. Then we were saved! And we go through that process. Did you know that righteous people can fall? We are human. But we have God to meet us there and we don't stay down. The bible says in Proverbs 24:17, "For though the righteous fall seven times, they rise again, but the wicked stumble when calamity strikes!"

You have two choices…either you fall backwards and backslide or you fall forward and continue in the journey- that's progress! In life we will all have troubles come our way. Calamity falls on the just and the unjust. Life is just life. We will each have similar struggles. The differences are the solutions we choose!

In all four gospels and all accounts are the fall of Peter. Jesus tells him… "YOU WILL FALL!" Then most certainly, his denial of Jesus Christ is written four times. There is power of choice! Your outcome doesn't have to be that way.

Peter messes up and weeps.

Judas messes up and hangs.

Peter was a bold man, a very vocal individual, expressive and outspoken. Yet many of us are like this and we get in trouble just by being so expressive and emotional.

But Peter got up! He met Jesus again and WAITED for the promise! Falling forward is admission – humility – surrender – acceptance. It is promptly acting upon that issue. On many instances we are afraid to admit our weakness when we fall because we will be judged. We need that safe place… Jesus is it! We need a place where we can be free, protected, empowered, **renewed** and strengthened. There has to be a place and platform to grow so that we get to that ultimate purpose.

Suzanne Eller wrote in The Mended Heart,

"Why is the church not a safe place to talk about our struggles and receive grace and support in a loving community."

Jesus set the love – He raised the standards.

I want to raise the standards too!

> ***But go, tell his disciples AND Peter 'He is going ahead of you into Galilee. There you will see Him, just as He told you.'*** Mark 16:7 (New International Version)

Do we expect it to be so easy? NO!

The bible says that Peter wept bitterly! A sign of utter brokenness. The book of Mark says he broke down and wept. As he recalled the words of Jesus, "You Will Fall Away!"

In the Gospel of Luke, we see the power of God's saving strength and purpose.

> ***"Simon, Simon, Satan has ASKED to sift all of you as wheat. But I prayed for you Simon, that your faith may not fail and when you have turned back, STRENGTHEN YOUR BROTHERS!"*** Luke 22:31 (New International Version)

Purpose!

Everyone will be sifted...it wasn't just for Peter. He is just showing us through the scriptures that He does see that one! Don't hang yourself spiritually. Don't kill your purpose. As the enemy comes to bring that shame, guilt and rejection, God came to give you His GRACE, love and redemption!

He came back and strengthened his brothers and sisters!

How did he get to be the powerful Apostle Peter in the book of Acts… Jesus reinstates him in John 21:15-17, for every call, to cancel the fall.

"Simon son of John, do you love me more than these?"

"Yes Lord."

"Do you love me?"

"Yes Lord."

"Do you love me"

Peter was able to recover from that fall.

He fell forward into the perfect place for God to move.

So can you and I… no more relapse!

Gospel accounts of Peter as referenced above:

Matthew 26:31
Mark 14:27
Luke 22:31-34
John 13:38
Matthew 26:69-75
Mark 14:66-72
Luke 22:54-62
John 18:15-18, 25-27

REBUILT: Beginning the Ending

PIECE 10

WHERE IS YOUR SUPPORT SYSTEM

TRUST! Oh wow, what a concept. This is part of the healing process. Where we begin to trust people again or gain back the trust of others from damage we ourselves have caused. We all need a good support system and in becoming new, it helps to have new friends too. Good friends. Since we have been previously hurt, we put up that wall of Berlin quickly!

> *I am a companion of all who fear you and of those who keep Your precepts.* Psalm 119:63 (New King James Version)

These are the kind of friends that we have to have in our life if we want to continue in a new life. Those we can trust. Unfortunately, in this life we have experienced our shares of hardships in this area and it does not mean that there is no one else left to trust. You can find trust in the right people. Especially in those that have an intimate relationship with Christ. The fruit in them will show that.

Cut off what is toxic and keep what is treasure.

Trust is belief that someone or something is reliable, good, honest, effective, etc.

Isn't it funny how we can all suffer with the Thomas syndrome? Like we have to see it to believe it!

We've been hurt so bad that now we don't trust ANYONE... and that is a hard place to be if you think about it. Holding onto pain, putting up walls and barriers and making a serious check list...that is a lot of work. Of course we have to be mindful in relationships but when trust is trying to be established and created with a green light, why do we struggle with that?

Wouldn't it be easier if we just got along?

God, You are my friend right?
Closed in...I feel it.
I need someone to talk to.
Someone I can trust.
Someone that knows me.
Someone that will listen.
Someone that will guide me.
Especially when I need it the most.
This is so difficult. Hard to handle.

You're my friend right?

I think You are... based on Your word...You stick closer than a brother.

I need more than a brother now.

Where Is Your Support System

I need some support and serious guidance.
Especially when my mind goes crazy because of things!
Things happen and they go out of control, but why?
Why does this happen? Why do the little things stir up a pot to become big things?

Is it even necessary? I know there is a way…a better way. You are that way and I am running to You this way because it is the only way that I know.

I have experienced so much in this life.
I hate the saying, "Trust NO one" but I do get to that point.
Who do I trust?
Who can I turn to?
Who can help me here? In the darkest hour when good occurs something quickly comes to distort. I have great friends and I prayed for them ALL. I didn't want anyone led in my life that wasn't sent by You. Especially when I came to the Light. That light was You so I knew. I would ask You for even this.

One time I wrote with a tear stained face in a cold hallow building…the sermon was continuing… I begged You. I said, "God please! Send me someone or I will die."

I was sent the best thing ever. One I thought was a friend and was not. It was an adversary…to buffet me. To destroy me. To kill me. What was I sent? Jesus I need a friend. From the depths of my soul, I cry out and I need You more than anything in this earth. For all else has fallen and failed. I promised You that I would give it all. Until the point that I thought I would die for real. I pleaded, "Keep me alive!"

And You kept me alive by Your word and by Your promise. I trusted You when I could trust none. You know the depths of my soul and it bleeds. It bleeds so bad that it hurts! I can feel the pain still. And I know that You know. I know that You know me. I know You have the answer. For I cry out. I need that love from You. The love from the "bestest" friend in the world that won't destroy me but will BUILD me and understand every ounce of me. For when it hurts so badly I know You are there… You are the friend.

You are the One and there will NEVER be another…I know that from the depth of my being.

> ***My heart is overflowing with a good theme; I recite my composition concerning the King; My tongue is the pen of a ready writer.*** Psalm 45:1 (New King James Version)

For my tongue is the pen of a ready writer and I will write this way to You because You know me and this is the way I can express me… to save some including myself! This brings me life. It is a haven for me and a place of rest. A place that I know will be recorded for good. It is my place… YOU are my friend.

This is my cry, this is my prayer. For when all else dies, this is all that will live. You are my friend. I think in all that I have learned is to be stripped of all until I knew that You were IT.

> ***To whom then will you liken God? Or what likeness will you compare to Him?*** Isaiah 40:18 (New King

James Version)

"To whom then will you liken Me, Or to whom shall I be equal?" says the Holy One. Isaiah 40:25 (New King James Version)

Oh Lord there is NONE like YOU!!!!
You were the only One and from the very beginning.
My Friend indeed.
My Source.
My Deliver.
My Redeemer.
My Counselor.
My Life.
My Helper.
My Encourager.
You are it all.

Now I know… Jesus You are my friend.
I need someone to talk to. I need my friend God, You are it, right!
Yes, You are.
It's okay, I love You too… thank You for being YOU!

PROVERBS 18 (New Living Translation)

Unfriendly people care only about themselves;
they lash out at common sense.
Fools have no interest in understanding;
they only want to air their own opinions.
Doing wrong leads to disgrace,
and scandalous behavior brings contempt.
Wise words are like deep waters;

wisdom flows from the wise like a bubbling brook.
It is not right to acquit the guilty
or deny justice to the innocent.
Fools' words get them into constant quarrels;
they are asking for a beating.
The mouths of fools are their ruin;
they trap themselves with their lips.
Rumors are dainty morsels
that sink deep into one's heart.
A lazy person is as bad as
someone who destroys things.
The name of the LORD is a strong fortress;
the godly run to him and are safe.
The rich think of their wealth as a strong defense;
they imagine it to be a high wall of safety.
Haughtiness goes before destruction;
humility precedes honor.
Spouting off before listening to the facts
is both shameful and foolish.
The human spirit can endure a sick body,
but who can bear a crushed spirit?
Intelligent people are always ready to learn.
Their ears are open for knowledge.
Giving a gift can open doors;
it gives access to important people!
The first to speak in court sounds right—
until the cross-examination begins.
Flipping a coin can end arguments;
it settles disputes between powerful opponents.
An offended friend is harder to win back than a fortified city.
Arguments separate friends like a gate locked with bars.

Wise words satisfy like a good meal;
the right words bring satisfaction.
The tongue can bring death or life;
those who love to talk will reap the consequences.
The man who finds a wife finds a treasure,
and he receives favor from the LORD.
The poor plead for mercy;
the rich answer with insults.
There are "friends" who destroy each other,
but a real friend sticks closer than a brother.

Jesus... YOU ARE MY FRIEND!

I have a partner! Isn't that amazing? I am not alone. A lie keeps repeating in my head that I have to cancel out so often and remind myself that I have a permanent partner in life that is never going to leave me or forsake me. We are in this together. God has tremendous plans for us. After your season of suffering, God in all His grace will **restore**, confirm, strengthen and establish you". 1 Peter 5:10

I am thinking about this "new" concept called HOPE. For some time I really lost that. I lost my hope, my love, my passion, my zest and zeal for life. Restoration sounded impossible. Then I kept going despite all the troubled feelings I had. Despite all the work it was taking me to salvage up any life that may have been left. But God was right about one thing mainly (as He is always correct). He wanted to remind me that I didn't have to look anymore. That I didn't have to search. That I didn't have to try so hard but that it was truly a time for REST in my life! I just needed the right partner- GOD.

This rest that I speak of is not the kind that is absent of physical labor because I am a busy person as a wife, mom, full-time worker and pastor…but rest [the refreshing quiet; relief or freedom, especially from anything that wearies, troubles, or disturbs] in a different place. I am now brought to a place where I rest in HIS presence and knowing that He really does have my back. I never been so close with Him and understanding that He reminded me, "There are so many women back home waiting for you so what are YOU WAITING FOR!?! Redirect yourself! Refocus yourself! REVIVE! RENEW! RESTORE! REBUILD! I am there … I always have been."

I decided to finally accept an offer to go to the gym for a game of doubles racquetball. I used to always play but gave up this sport all together because it got so dangerous. I did not want to go because of the fear of being hit. That fear is just so present that all could feel it. I have a great partner named Dan that keeps going no matter what. He kept telling me, "Take that fear out of your mind and just play your game." Since it has been so long, I kept making so many mistakes too. I told him, "I am making too many mistakes!!!" He said, **"There is NO too many mistakes!"** I thought to myself these words are beyond powerful, he has no idea how much they are impacting my life right now.

That is the same way with God. He is our best partner. He keeps encouraging us, helping us and reminding us to keep going. As humans we then remind Him of our mistakes when He is not doing that with us. He is reminding us of our future always not the past. He says the same things to us when we keep telling Him how many mistakes we make!!! He says, "My Grace is sufficient for thee [2 Corinthians 12:9]." His love covers a multitude of sins [Proverbs 10:12]. So I don't have to keep reminding myself of mistakes but reminding myself of God's love for me. These guys were so happy to have me there playing with them. Another said to me after I told him how bad that I did, "Give yourself credit for getting back on the court that is not easy. Glad to see you still have that competitive spirit." So I played being afraid until that feeling went away. Just need more getting used to all this again. Time will help. With Dan as my partner, we won!

The growing weeks of recovery has been such a blessing for me [bitter, sweet] to receive precious moments of encouragement. My spiritual mommy is here and says to me, "You look less stressed!" That a good friend can tell me, "You don't need the counselor anymore –God is your counselor, go to Him!" That a good book can remind me to stop trying so hard and recognize how much God loves me despite all of my past- IT IS GONE! I have to move forward! There is a future He is waiting to release to me. Written by Suzanne Eller, "But in reality, the most powerful act we can do is to rest in what He's already done for us. It's a foundation upon which all other change can be built."

I go to church and see so many smiley faces of sisters that have respect for me. Sisters that encourage me. Sisters that don't talk about me but pray for me! Sisters that want the best for me. All of this just makes me smile. But most of all that God is picking up the pieces of something that He always saw so precious… my daughter Cassandra Isabella Mendez. I wish I could tell you all that He is doing it? But just know that HE IS A RESTORER OF ALL THINGS! I have never been so thankful of my family of 4, my family of sisterhood and family in church at MUI. God loves me and loves you. Just do what I did…. I just said "YES Lord! Take it all…take my life…I am your vessel indeed." This is a major reason I built my blog site "juschrist4.com" to reflect my built family. I have an amazing Partner and I am not giving Him up for anything!

You will find that friend that loves at all times! Believe it!

I love that scripture because it bears so much truth.

Friends never change with each other. They grow with each other. Time is meaningful, always worthwhile. There is never envy, but rejoicing within. You're never afraid to be yourself. You share what's on your heart. Trust is present and never any doubt. When they speak, you learn even more. They teach you something valuable. Time passes so quickly when you are with them because you are not mindful of your clock. Boredom doesn't exist ever because there is always something to share. Even silence is golden. Just sharing one by one. If time has passed between them, it never hinders the friendship. Smiles are exchanged. Love is always present. They encourage one another. And they are not afraid to be weaker. For words to uplift will always spill through.

Where Is Your Support System

I have very few of these and they know who they are. They are my family, they spent years learning of me, and they never judged me in anyway or spread any evil word. They supported me throughout my life and I am forever grateful. They called me a friend and showed me that they meant it. It is not a relationship where I only give, for even if I couldn't they understood that all the more. They gave to me more than I could expect. They stood in the gap for me, prayed for me, warred with me, knew all my ups and downs and kept it just for us. That is the friend that is so lifelong. The work that is cultivated goes for us all. We all give and we all take, there is more every time and nothing less than that.

They don't lie to me. They don't get mad at me like that. They don't feel threatened by me or have to compete. Why would they if they are my friend, for it is iron that sharpens iron [Proverbs 27:17]? I will never forget the conversations, the times they heard me cry, share or vent. The times I felt like giving up, for all they could tell me was keep moving, keep believing. When my heart was heavy they felt it too. It was a shared pain not only for me to bear. They took the time through all that too. They heard me laugh. They know my story. Nothing is hidden because I know I can tell it. I also know their story for they also shared with me. To encourage me and let me know, they needed me as well.

I counted them by hand, yes only just a few…
Thank you!!!
Thank you for giving me FAITH!

Thank you for giving me HOPE!
Thank you for giving me LOVE!
For when I thought those things could never exist again… You pointed me back to the one who could give it.

You helped lead me back to GOD!!!

So I will never forget.

WHEN YOU NEED IT THE MOST, GOD IS THERE… and you can find the friend in God. There is always that one good friend and you know it by the fruit of them.

Trust can be granted again.

I know these pieces are deep, strong, intimate and personal. But they were all written during the first few months of my renewal. They make this book a reality. They make this book a testimony. They make this book a transparent view that we all go through it and we can be renewed.

Our first tendency will always be that of Thomas—that we need to see to believe. In this life we need to walk it to believe it. Even when nothing else makes sense. Rational doesn't always play a role…it is our faith that will.

Now let's move on to our process of restoration.

RESTORE

To bring back into existence, use, or the like; reestablish- to bring back to a former state- originate or normal condition as building; to bring back to a state of health, soundness or vigor (become alive); to put back to a former place or to a former position or bank. To give back; to reproduce or reconstruct, make return or restitution of (anything taken away or lost).

Bring back
Build up
Cure
Heal
Improve
Make healthy
Make restitution
Mend
Recall
Recondition
Reconstruct
Recover
Redeem
Refurbish
Renew
Renovate
Repair
Rescue
Retouch
Revive
Strengthen

Touch up
Update
Win back

"For the gifts and the calling of God are irrevocable"
Romans 11:29 (New King James Version)

PIECE 11

LOVE NEVER FAILS

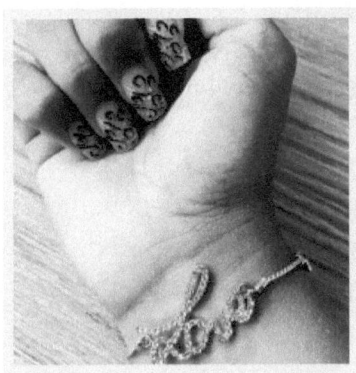

A little reminder on my wrist, I cherish this little bracelet, that says in script the one thing that will never fail – L O V E! Which I now makes the only permanent mark I have and I am more than okay with that. There are things that I have done far worse than this and are erasable by the power of His blood.

In order to be restored – LOVE must cover us. Several

times in experiencing brokenness, we had come to recognize that we had lost this at some point. This causes heartbreak, pain and loss. We end up spending so much time running from life because we are grieving. No one likes to grieve but it is necessary to pass through any form of loss. We lose validation, trust, friends, family, finances, opportunities and so many other sources that we had at one point heavily relied upon.

I know that in my writings I can be very raw and perhaps many will not approve. But this is my story. This was a mandate to release the words in this book. As I found healing, so will many others. This is my testimony that I am sharing with those that I know need to hear it. The scars that I thought would mark me in the worst way became testimonies of how God continuously came through for me.

I will repeat the words of a new covenant brother in Christ as he encouraged me and shared, "Only one who is restored can be a restorer. That's why it had to be you," Apostle Femi Adun.

Listen the world is not perfect and neither shall we ever be. That is why we ALL need a savior. But when you are broken, you need the healer! You need the helper to cover you. That is what I found. In hurting people, in hurting myself and putting such a huge dent in my sphere I had to know that there was something and someone that I could turn to FIRST! I am thankful that my immediate family had received me…they were hurt but they received me. I am thankful that God led me to good friends and counselors to breathe back life into me. There is nothing wrong with seeking help! We need that! And if you feel like you're going crazy then seek professional help too! Whatever it takes to get you to wholeness, use it! Don't feel bad about that for one minute. I had professional counseling for two years. I seek counsel STILL from trusted mentors and others that I know are stronger in areas that I lack. This is all a matter of perception. Seeking counsel doesn't mean you are crazy, it means you consciously recognize you need help.

This way when you bounce back you will see how you are going to be a strong source for others too. God uses all these situations to strengthen us that we may live a victorious life. The love that He demonstrated for us to get there is the door we walk through to begin that restoration process. I am eternally gratefully that I came to truly embrace and understand the love of God during a time like this.

Your expectation for restoration will not just come from people. They will not be all of it for you. It is just a help. They are not perfect. We all fall short. I will never be everything for someone and they will never be everything for me. God will be everything for EVERYONE. With all our broken pieces we come together to be made whole.

Let's not lose sight of this truth.

Because His love is greater!

Every time we put that love into the hands and trust of others, we give them the power to destroy us... and if you love them enough you can trust that they won't. The reality is that it will happen when people do not meet all of our expectations.

This message that I share is not geared to the one that is righteous, the one that has it all together, the one that already won the battle and is standing valiantly and triumphantly. Everyone has their own story of how they conquered. This is for the one that is seeking validation and understanding just as I did! This is for the one that needs to be restored right now or needs that constant reminder.

If you were broken, torn, rejected, abandoned, sinful, hurtful, angry, tormented, hated, afraid, depressed, dying, cheated on, lied to or betrayed then this message IS for you. This pain can hit the heights especially when it is done by those closest to us and we are standing there asking, "WHY? Why God?"

I lived that life. I was not perfect and I am not ashamed to share what God has *freed* me from. I suffered with many addictions and struggles and that left me to search for comfort in every other place that was apart from the ways of God. Yes—even AS a Christian because I was also one that was hurt by Christians! I rebelled. I didn't know how to cope and accept that they too needed redemption. I came from a very dark past and when I got to the church instead of things getting lighter for me they got darker.

You know for too long we allow people to manipulate, criticize and destroy us. The enemy will use anyone to do that with you. Be free of that manipulating and critical spirit! Don't give room or permission for someone to bombard you with their own personal convictions, ways of doing things and rules—seek God for that! You are different and will have another means of doing things that work best for you. And it will be right, when you do it God's way!

I remember one day sitting in a church and hearing the preacher share on forgiveness. I sat there in uncontrollable tears once again as he looked me square in the eye summarizing these words, "Forgive them, because it will only allow you the freedom to forgive yourself. You are there so that God can use that opportunity to display His love."

They also are not perfect and I had to find a way to love those that hurt me as well. This is a part of us maturing in our walk with the Lord. That piece will need to be strengthened for us as well. Or we will be year after year carrying pains and becoming bitter for things we have done or what was done to us. We must let go.

I needed to recover from all the hurt that everyone in all my life had caused me. I needed love, forgiveness and that redemptive power that only Christ could bring me in a perfect way.

I have been through men. I have been through the drugs. I have been through the alcohol. I have been through the suicide thoughts and attempts. I have been through the running. I have been through the carousing. I have been through all of that and yes in the church I did all of that too.

But God set me apart. God snatched me from living that type of life. He freed me and forgave me. Now I live for Him. I live a life of recovery.

Who is to say I would not fall again? Could I? Certainly! We all can be susceptible. But I am not pressing for that, cultivating that, entertaining that or living for that. Changes were made in my life whether I wanted them or not. All vulnerabilities are surrendered to God. That is a must.

I want a happy family—in Christ.
I want my children to love and respect me—in Christ.
I want my husband to love me unconditionally—in Christ.
I want my brothers and sisters to see me as integral—in Christ.

And so I canceled out everything that was a hindrance. It has been one of the deepest years in my life now. I DON'T want to mess that up for anyone—most importantly, myself. Because the one that it impacted the most was ME! I don't want to hurt or hinder my relationship with God. I came this far and I am going to remain in His presence.

Just as David wrote in Psalm 51:4, "Against you, you only, have I sinned and done what is evil in your sight; so you are right in your verdict and justified when you judge."

We are not going back! I am not going back. I do remember rock bottom!!! But I also remember meeting Jesus Christ, my rock, my fortress, my savior and my deliver RIGHT AT THAT BOTTOM. I am able to be thankful and grateful for His saving strength. I am okay with admitting that I am weak. I am okay with admitting where I need to be strengthened. If I was not weak, I would never be able to experience the *strength* of God. And that is what I see evident in my life now. That is what counts. Because of the love of God.

He recovered us to get us into recovery!
"New Day New Me Recovery Journal" by Mike Shea

Who will validate you?
God will! Every single time!

So don't worry if you are not as perfect as the rest. Maybe you are filled with tattoos, piercings, a history of violence and abandonment. Maybe you have several kids outside of wedlock. Maybe you are not married and have lost your purity. Maybe you are the one that has experienced every drug under the sun. Maybe you have been married more than once. Maybe you have been the one that was an adulterer or the one cheated on. Maybe you are the one that is uneducated and collecting government help! SO WHAT!!!! Did God not come for all those things? Did God not come PRECISELY for that? He did not come for the righteous my friend, He came for you!!! He came to bring us repentance.

If other people have it already –the home in place, the marriage, the stationed job and bank account in order, fresh clean skin and not a single piercing. If they never tried the cig, swig or trick—and you did, don't put your focus on that. If they have what looks to you as all together lovely, trust me that they needed help too. Everyone needs a savior. Please be free in that and start learning how to celebrate the person that God made you to be and the person that He is working so diligently to restore! He is bringing you BACK! Back to life. Because His love and covering will never steer you wrong. If He did it with others, He will do it with you. Your time is here for recovery, you need to latch onto that. Receive His grace. Accept the love that was poured out. His love restores us.

I have been restored by that love and you can be restored by that love as well.

Love is indispensable.

> ***Love is patient, love is kind. It does not envy. It does not boast. It is not proud. It does not dishonor others, it is not self-seeking, it is not easily angered, it keeps no record of wrongs. Love does not delight in evil but rejoices with the truth. It always protects, always trusts, always hopes, always perseveres. Love NEVER fails. But where there are prophecies they will cease; where there are tongues, they will be stilled; where there is knowledge, it will all pass away.*** 1 Corinthians 13:4-8 (New International Version)

Christian Love—The Highest and Best Gift

> *If I speak with the eloquence of men and of angels, but have no love, I become no more than blaring brass or crashing cymbal. If I have the gift of foretelling the future and hold in my mind not only all human knowledge but the very secrets of God, and if I also have*

that absolute faith which can move mountains, but have no love, I amount to nothing at all. If I dispose of all that I possess, yes, even if I give my own body to be burned, but have no love, I achieve precisely nothing. This love of which I speak is slow to lose patience—it looks for a way of being constructive. It is not possessive: it is neither anxious to impress nor does it cherish inflated ideas of its own importance. Love has good manners and does not pursue selfish advantage. It is not touchy. It does not keep account of evil or gloat over the wickedness of other people. On the contrary, it is glad with all good men when truth prevails. Love knows no limit to its endurance, no end to its trust, no fading of its hope; it can outlast anything. It is, in fact, the one thing that still stands when all else has fallen. 1 Corinthians 13:1-8, J.B. Phillips New Testament (PHILLIPS)

The first time I heard this translation, I was listening to a message on the radio by Corrie Ten Boom. I was driving on my way to work and will never forget how impacting this message was. I shared it with a lot of people after hearing. She spoke about her testimony during the time of the Holocaust. She read this scripture of 1 Corinthians 13 after testifying how the Lord had to do such a work in her heart. She had to extend this love to the ones that brought on death and torture to many. She said 97,000 women died, including her sister. She was a survivor of the Holocaust and able to preach the Word of God to many. One day after preaching on forgiveness and love, a soldier approached her and asked if she would do the same even for him. In that moment she remembered an evil man that caused such torment. Yet he reached out his hand for a handshake and she said she didn't know how she did it but truly the love of God manifested as she shook his hand. In that moment, she experienced forgiveness and love all over again. She lived the word that she preached.

Corrie stated, "When we can't love in the old human way, God can give us the *perfect* way. Do you know what hurts us so very much? *It's love*. Love is the strongest force in the world, and when it is blocked that means pain. There are two things we can do when this happens. We can kill that love so that it stops hurting. But then of course part of us dies too. Or we can ask God **to *open up a healthy route*** for that love to travel." God showed us this love. He has poured out His love and given to us an outpouring of the greatest gift that could ever exist. This other route is THROUGH God! This is the best love!

Love is what we seek. Love is what we respond to. Love is what we crave. Love is what moves us. Love is what touches us. Love is what keeps us alive. Love is what causes the greatest pain when it is shut out. We experience that in human form -a **FLAWED** love. So God **exchanges** it for His **unfailing love**! This is the love that will never fail us. This is the love that will outlast all. Just as the opening scripture declares – it is the one thing that will still stand when all else has fallen. This gives us hope. This makes us trust again. This makes us build again when something was broken. There is a way. That way is through God. I find no other way to have such a joy and freedom. Give love a chance. Give God a chance.

This love is what He wants us to practice with others despite what has happened to us. We still walk in love, we choose love, we surrender to love and we follow love for GOD IS LOVE. We shall not be afraid of the risk.

> ***"He who does not love does not know God, for God is love."*** 1 John 4:8 (New King James Version)

> ***"There is no fear in love; but perfect love casts out fear, because fear involves torment. But he who fears has not been made perfect in love."*** 1 John 4:18 (New King James Version)

> ***"Therefore, as the elect of God, holy and beloved, put on tender mercies, kindness, humility, meekness, longsuffering; bearing with one another, and forgiving one another, if anyone has a complaint against another; even as Christ forgave you, so you also must do. But above all these things put on love, which is the bond of perfection."*** Colossians 3:12-14 (New King James Version)

If you don't know what to do at this point of your life, receive the love of God. That is always available for you first. His love is what will uncover us to experience freedom, it will cover us by validation, recover us from anything that has broken us and we will finally discover our purpose through Him.

If you do find this to be something difficult then ask God for the help. He has given us the Helper – Holy Spirit to lead us in this. We shall be able to do all things through Him…. even love in the midst of any circumstance. Use the Word. You will find as you read through the passages of scripture, there is an underlying theme of love that has the power to restore and rebuild you.

God will love you and appreciate you more than any man or woman on this earth. In His eyes He finds you precious. That is your validation.

That is the way. Take this way.

L <3 V E

For I am the Lord your God,
The Holy One of Israel, your Savior;
I give Egypt for your ransom,
Cush and Seba in your stead.
Since **you are precious**
and **honored** in my sight,
and because **I love you**.
Isaiah 43:3-4 (NIV)

PIECE 12
I NEED A COVER

I am always reflecting on just how much I need God in my life. How much I need Him as my cover. I am always cognizant and thinking of how most women in particular always seem to have some sort of heart issue the most. I reflect on how David wrote in Psalm 23:1, "The Lord is my Shepherd, I shall not be in want." For if he had the Lord present with him throughout his life, why should he have a "want". He is covered in every way. All the covers we need to be strong in the Lord and in the power of His might. Everyone has this matter of the heart. We need a cover.

- ☐ **Cover**
- ☐ **Recover**
- ☐ **Discover**
- ☐ **Uncover**

How much those words do bring meaning to my life. For it

is God that is covering me now like a shield. He is my **cover** [to place something over or upon, as for protection, concealment or warmth].

Through God I am able to **recover** [to get back, return to a normal state of health, mind or strength].

With God I have been able to **discover** [To see and get knowledge of, learn of, find out; discern, notice or realize] why I am here and who I am in Christ.

Finally, I can freely testify that God was able to **uncover** [to lay bar, disclose, reveal, remove the covering] of anything in my life that was such a hindrance to me. Just as a wound exposed needs the air to bring on the covering of a scab for protection and new growth – is the same way God does with us when the wounds are uncovered. We uncover so we can get back the real cover we need.

The covering of God.

With that covering we can do so much. I saw the movie, "Southpaw" and the agent had to remind the fighter, "Every time you thought you couldn't get up…. You got up!" And this is true. He took on the next fight. Kept it moving. I loved that movie. It was such a powerful act of character with many impacting words. For we always tend to first think that we CAN'T! But we do it.

For all the blows of life that come to us, He reminds us that He is our **shield**. We just get back up EVERY time! "But you, Lord, are a shield around me, my glory, the One who lifts my head high." Psalm 3:3

He covers us. He lifts us up. It is a new time in life for rebirth and growth. New places and new ventures. He makes all things new…that is His promise to us during our restoration.

All I can say is I am amazed to see all the ones around me growing too. Through good times and bad this is what we call really pushing through! A leader among leaders is what we shall be and I can't express enough how the words of many have been such an encouragement to my life. How those powerful words have influenced me! There are so many times I share a word too and I feel every word in that sermon. I live every word… people have no idea just how much and I wish I could share all of my painful processes without distorting the minds of people. But it is that mind-distorting thing that only my God knows all too well. In time yes, I will give more and that is why He leads me to a written platform like this. I want to share and need to but just know that this process is painful, there is no doubt about that one. But we all find our **purpose** in that pain…we all find God's **presence** in that pain… and we will all find our **power** that God gives us in that pain! Sometimes we can feel so powerless over our situation, but that situation is perfect because that is the place of complete control in God.

I finished reading the 12 Step recovery book/bible… it is not that we all have experienced alcohol or drug addictions but that we become addicted to something! That "thing" brings us through that process over and over again. Remember an addiction is ANYTHING that you are enslaved to a habit or practice something that is psychologically or physically **habit-forming,** LIKE narcotics, to the extent that its cessation (complete stopping) causes severe trauma. Maybe you were addicted to a drug, a drink, a relationship, a friend, or any lifestyle apart from Christ…whatever that had you feeling high and comfortable on a high horse. It is only a matter of time that you come down to reality, the "honeymoon phase" is over, the high is gone, the moment has ended, when you lost everything and have nothing left. It is there at this moment that God meets you!

I read something that I wrote months back during my trauma. I had to make a sacrifice. I had to surrender all.

I stated, "I hate to do this, but God loves it." This just reminded me. I must stay the course.

Remember that trauma stage, this is NOT a bad thing. From where God took you. Just remember it well, so that you are familiar with the stronghold and will be able to conquer it even more if it tries to come back. Take 1 Samuel Chapters 22- 30 to study and observe the life of this man David. He suffered much but his victory was amazing!!! And that can be us too. As for myself I have no followers now. I have sisters, I have family, I have disciples, other leaders to bear the burdens with and I know I am not alone. Just as God has led me here to this point to know this. This is my life now, *a surrendered one*! And if He had to strip me of all that to get me here today then so be it. I have no choice and when I have no choice I make the commitment. I need no more but God and He will lead me to and through the rest! I had to go through the covers so that I can experience the ultimate covering during my recovery.

Recovery is possible!

I don't exactly know what the problem is, else call it an addiction.

What is your addiction? What is calling you back? What is constantly waging war against your soul and entire being?

What has been so habit-forming in your life that needs to be broken off completely?

So many forms when no one else sees, a force so strong…to fight every single day!

How do we get back to life when we think that one thing will do it all?

It's just one reach away. To step into a swirl of the forbidden. The thing you feel will bring the life, dull the pain and heal the wound.

In one moment –

It is taking another shot of that vodka.

It is taking another drag of that smoke.

It is taking another one of those pills.

It is taking another sting of that needle.

It is being naked in that room.

It is feeling the colored blade mark the tat.

It is feeling the razor cut the skin.

It is going back to that bad relationship.

It is placing another bet at that casino.

It is going back to that store to spend money.

Why do we keep going back to things that are making us MISERABLE anyway? STOP!!! HOW? GET THE HELP THAT YOU NEED!!!!!

For addiction comes in many forms –do not be deceived. If you struggle to break it or break through then it IS an addiction! It is like you can't even function without it. You don't know how to cope, what to do, where to go or what to say. But I am here to tell you today that there is a way!

There is a way beyond all of this. **Free** from addiction. **Free** from habit-forming destruction. **Free** from enslavement. **Free** from bondage. The way to be free is through HIM! He is the One that will set us free–we just have to give this to Him entirely and every day of our life!

> *Jesus said, "I tell you most solemnly that anyone who chooses a life of sin is trapped in a dead-end life and is, in fact, a slave. A slave is a transient, who can't come and go at will. The Son, though, has an established position, the run of the house. So if the Son sets you free, you are free through and through."* John 8:34-36 (The Message)

He is the One that will bring you back to life – a life through Him. A life through prayer. A life through His word. A life of worship. A life of truth. He has all of that–a natural and lasting high if you stick with it. The same way you reached out for other things now is the time to reach out to the King of kings!!! BREAK OFF THE ADDICTION! BREAK PAST IT THROUGH HIS WORD! BREAK PAST IT THROUGH THE POWER OF HIS PRESENCE AND THROUGH THE POWER OF HIS REDEMPTION!

BREAK!
BREAK!
BREAK!

Be consistent with God and lose the consistency of the addiction.

> *"So let's not allow ourselves to get fatigued doing good. At the right time we will harvest a good crop if we don't give up, or quit. Right now, therefore, every time we get the chance, let us work for the benefit of all, starting with the people closest to us in the community of faith."*
> ~Galatians 6:9-10 (The Message)

It is not hard to break if you use the best source! The best help, the best support, the best gift that was given to us in order to be free and live in abundance.

> "God can do anything, you know—far more than you could ever imagine or guess or request in your wildest dreams! He does it not by pushing us around

but by working within us, His Spirit deeply and gently within us.
Glory to God in the church!
Glory to God in the Messiah, in Jesus!
Glory down all the generations!
Glory through all millennia! Oh, yes!" Ephesians 3: 20-21 (The Message)

That one thing that you think will bring you back to life in the moment you reach for it is not the habit…it is not the thing…it is not the drug, it is not the drag, it is neither the alcohol or the boy next store! It is simply the One that was meant to fill every void.

Everyone has an addiction in some way, shape or form. I have plenty of my own and I bring it before my KING! When I feel the onset of the battle coming upon me – I reach, I stretch… not for the thing but for the King and He ALWAYS takes me through it!

Exchange that reach. Stretch your faith. Go reach for Him. It will bring you back to the best LIFE ever…it's everlasting life!

> *Jesus answered and said to her, "Whoever drinks of this water will thirst again, but whoever drinks of the water that I shall give him will never thirst. But the water that I shall give him will become in him a fountain of water springing up into everlasting life." John 4:13-14 (New King James Version)*

I used to think that recovery wasn't possible. When I

messed up or had been through the worst of the worst, I always thought that it was over for me. We call that "rock bottom."

Problem is–I hit rock bottom a lot and practically daily to the point that my rock bottom became my addiction. It was a habit. A bondage. A stronghold over me. A grip so tight that it was tormenting. I had no control over my situation, so I thought! But that was and is never the case with God!

When you encounter those rock bottom moments, God promises that He can fill you, renew you and change you forever so that you win! That you have power–YES! Power over your addiction! Power to overcome the problem! Power to progress! Now you just live by the process of renewal which is called a new life! Where all things become new.

> ***Therefore, if anyone is in Christ, he is a new creation; old things have passed away; behold, all things have become new*** 2 Corinthians 5:17 (New King James Version)

Recovery is possible and it is also a lifestyle. You cannot practice the process of recovery for only a temporary time. The new life must become **permanent change**. It is an everyday life now.

There is hope! There is power over that addiction!

You CAN recover!

The problem is that people are not able to overcome their

dependencies because they are hiding it or trying to do this on their own strength. When you have a problem you need help right? So you must come to the Helper [Holy Spirit] so that He can direct you in all things and lead you to godly people to also help with that process.

Most CHRISTIANS are struggling with an addiction of some sort!

They are struggling because they hide it too–just like anyone with an addiction. They are afraid to tell someone for fear of judgement. But if you want to get well then tell!!! Obviously not one that shows fruits of barbaric judgement but godly people to help support you. James 5:16 says, "Confess your trespasses to one another, and pray for one another, that you may be healed. The effective, fervent prayer of a righteous man avails much."

Get therapy. Check into a rehabilitation program. Tell your pastors. Seek leaders that can help or a support group where you can receive encouragement throughout your recovery process.

Don't avoid this — if you want to get well then you really must tell! And as technology is advancing, the techniques are also increasing to set the stage for sin. I am so sorry but I am not going to sugar coat the problems that are running rampant even throughout the church! Where men want to show you the "size of their prize" and women want to quickly display their "apple bottom" like the latest iPhone release!

Where are the morals here? Or the respect that we need as

an individual. You have a problem! And when you have a problem, you need help. The bible says that in the last days that even the elect will be deceived. Yes, the ELECT! The ones that are choice! The ones with strong callings! The ones in leadership roles. The enemy is moving fast to take down the best so he can be the best.

BUT WE WILL NOT LET THE ENEMY WIN!

Don't worry if your situation or addiction looks like it is not capable of recovery. Don't worry if you think that you feel too ashamed or that you are beyond repair, for it is at those precise times that God looks upon your situation and says, "PERFECT! This is EXACTLY why I sent my Son. They need saving and I am a Savior!"

There is a way to recover. You just need to SUBMIT to the steps. You can't be in the place of breakthrough only to return to that place of bondage. Remember –it is "All Things New!"

You know you have the problem. When you think those things can't be seen, they really are obvious that there is something incorrect. Be aware of your rock bottom problem.

Many instances we return back to the place where the dependencies are. We return back to the lifestyle. Surrounded by drugs, alcohol, sex, pornography, tobacco or anything that had you captive. Do some deep cleaning. If you want the change to really take place, then you will have to change things!!!

No going BACK!

If this is the way for you then you can start by deleting phone numbers, messages, pictures, toss the alcohol, lose the drugs, movies, websites, yes quit the relationship and make it so that THEY CAN'T FIND YOU!!! If this is a new you then they should not be able to easily find you to bind you! You have to get rid of all the dependencies that were contributing to your destruction.

YOU ARE IN RECOVERY!

Don't leave yourself vulnerable and susceptible to the enemy when you know you have a weakness!

Remember, this is not an easy walk but it is a walk that you are more than able and capable of doing. God will renew you, restore you and rebuild you. You just need to want it and follow through so that God has something to work with. Let Him create that PURE heart. Let Him renew a steadfast spirit within you. He won't cast you away and He won't leave you to do this alone!

You can and will be restored! And you will be able to help all those that suffer with things that you were able to conquer through God. Make the change. Find a good rehabilitation center for your particular struggle. Your situation is never beyond repair or fixing. There is help available. Pursue it, stretch out for help and admit when you need it.

He is going to give you all the covering that you need. Start by checking into God's rehabilitation center. The hotline

I Need A Cover

number to begin is 800-NO-GOING-BACK!

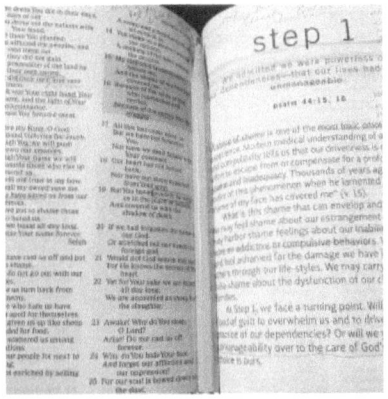

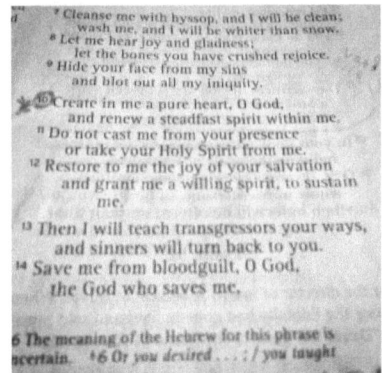

RECOVERY IS POSSIBLE!

Resources
Serenity: A Companion for Twelve Step Recovery
Authors, Robert Hemfelt and Richard Fowler.

REBUILT: Beginning the Ending

PIECE 13

HOPE FOR A TREE (LIKE ME)

"At least there is hope for a tree: If it is cut down, it will sprout again, and its new shoots will not fail. Its roots may grow old in the ground and its stump die in the soil, yet at the scent of water it will bud and put forth shoots like a plant. But a man dies and is laid low; he breathes his last and is no more. As the water of a lake dries up or a riverbed becomes parched and dry, so he lies down and does not rise; till the heavens are no more, people will not awake or be roused from their sleep. If only you would hide me in the grave and conceal me till your anger has passed! If only you would set me a time and then remember me! If someone dies, will they live again? All the days of my hard service I will wait for my renewal to come." Job 14:7-14

In the darkest hour of Job's life, he still had hope [the feeling that what is wanted can be had or that events will turn out for the best]. He believed that something would turn out for the best here in the midst of the worst pain in his life. He lost his property, his children and then his health. He had nothing left but a wife that told him to leave his faith! He had friends that told him he was a sinner! But most of all He had a God that was looking at him the entire time and waited for all this to pass. This simply was a test. For many of us, we go through testing in life. Some problems are actually brought our way to test our faith. Much like Abraham finally getting a promised son as an heir then being asked to sacrifice him [Genesis 22]! We don't always know why God allows certain situations to happen but the end result always proves something better and lasting. There are no accidents.

Job considered himself to be a tree. He saw himself as a strong person despite having been cut down almost next to nothing. There was hope. There was a shoot that would remain.

There was a shoot that would not fail. There was a part of Job that no matter how hard the blows of life came his way there was still something left. Passing through death, darkness, sickness and disease –he still felt there was something so deep and so rich that could never be taken away. That was his relationship with God. He was still going to talk to God. Whether he was happy or sad, glad or angry, with others or lonely, well or sick, with plenty or with none…Job was going to find the way to still get to the heart of God. He would not allow anything to stop his connection with God even when all else looked bleak. Job still found a way to pour out to the One that would make it better. Job still found a way to get to the One that was truly in control of his life. That was God.

Trees are strong. They have roots, depth, shape and longevity. That is the same way that we are in the faith. The same way we are when we keep a constant connection and relationship with the One who dwells in us –never leaving or forsaking us {Deuteronomy 31:6]. Even when the tree is cut there is something that remains. The core is still there. The roots are still dug in deep. There is still growth that could spring up. A tree will always remain. It is strong and can be immovable. In order for it to die it would have to be completely yanked out of the ground and pulled apart from its root. Our root and foundation is CHRIST. On Christ the solid rock we stand [Matthew 7:24] and everything else is just sinking sand.

At this point in my life, I can read this precious Word and receive this in the inner most part of me. I can say AT LEAST there is HOPE for a TREE [like me]. If I didn't have hope, I would have been crushed a long time ago and left this place. But my roots are seriously in Christ. I do have a new hope. There is a hope that does not disappoint when it is the one that is found through the love of God [Romans 5:5]! My relationship with God will never end. My circumstances in life will vary from day to day, some days more difficult than others but it is possible to get through them with God on my side. I am extremely thankful that He never left my side. He is my new hope. God is my best friend, the one that loves at all times. He is my husband. He is my counselor, my deliverer and my healer. He is everything that I will ever need in life. Everything else…is just an add on because of Him. My roots will never fail because they are deeper than they have ever been in my whole life. I wake with God, I talk with God, I cry with God, I laugh with God, I scream with God, I dance with God and now I write more because of God. This new life is with God and I shall hope to share it more in depth as I continue in my writing career.

Job declared, "I will wait for my renewal" and so it came. He had twice as much property in the end and had more beautiful children. The only difference was that his relationship with God was now more real! There are those that can speak the Word and others that will truly **live** it.

There is a tree planted by the rivers of water that brings forth its fruit in its season [Psalm 1]. This is the season that there is so much fruit. There is hope beyond measure!

Hope For A Tree (Like Me)

I pray that you believe that for you. That you still have an opportunity no matter how bad it looked. No matter how deep the cut, the wound, the hurt or the dirt. God came to take you out of that. Your focus and emphasis now needs to be God and you. Everything else follows after that. He picked you up and out of every mess. And if you are in a bigger mess now, it's okay because it is just a bigger test for God to be the best teacher of all. We will graduate with honors. We will soar like eagles. We will be used for His glory.

> *I will exalt you, Lord, for you lifted me out of the depths and did not let my enemies gloat over me. Lord my God, I called to you for help, and You healed me. You, Lord, brought me up from the realm of the dead; you spared me from going down to the pit.* Psalm 30:1-3 (New International Version)

Many times you will find yourself in a tight spot so that God can force you to go to a spacious place.

> *In you, Lord, I have taken refuge; let me never be put to*

shame; deliver me in your righteousness. Turn your ear to me, come quickly to my rescue; be my rock of refuge, a strong fortress to save me. Since you are my rock and my fortress, for the sake of your name lead and guide me. Keep me free from the trap that is set for me, for you are my refuge. Into your hands I commit my spirit; deliver me, Lord, my faithful God. I hate those who cling to worthless idols; as for me, I trust in the Lord. I will be glad and rejoice in your love, for you saw my affliction and knew the anguish of my soul. You have not given me into the hands of the enemy but have set my feet in a spacious place. Psalm 31:1-8 (New International Version)

Don't be discouraged. You will get through all the dark and weary days. God will take all the weak parts of you and pull them deep down into Him. You will conquer this thing! You will be that tree! You will be that one that has their roots the deepest. And the reward is the peace of God that will resonate from your every being.

Don't ever think that hope is lost! Have your hope anchored in Him. So that you become deep, strong and solid through Christ. That is what His word says in Psalm 1, "We shall be like a tree planted by the rivers of water bringing forth its fruit in its season."

PIECE 14
BEAUTY INSIDE

But the Lord said to Samuel, "Do not look at his appearance or at his physical stature, because I have refused him. For the Lord does not see as man sees; for man looks at the outward appearance, but the Lord looks at the heart." 1 Samuel 16:7 (New King James Version)

It is so funny how we make such quick decisions and come to conclusions just based on what we see on the outside. For some things appear unattractive, unappealing and so unapproachable. We avoid them but if we just step inside a thing and go a little further to see the core, it may just be the most beautiful thing you have seen or experienced ever.

Go a little further. Check inside…for there is a world of beauty in it that we would have never imagined possible just by what it looked like on the outside.

I took a trip to Bayard Cutting Arboretum State Park in Great River New York with 11 other ladies from our church for a brunch and tour. What a beautiful time we had have. I thought of nothing else but my current surroundings. I was at perfect peace looking around. This was an immaculate and exquisite place to visit. The place is known for its beauty with 691 acres of green land. So much to take in and view. It is surrounded by the Connetquot River, beautiful trees, pine, grass and more. The website provides this detail below:

Bayard Cutting Arboretum was donated to the Long Island State Park Region by Mrs. William Bayard Cutting and her daughter, Mrs. Olivia James, in memory of William Bayard Cutting, **"to provide an oasis of beauty and quiet for the pleasure, rest and refreshment of those who delight in outdoor beauty; and to bring about a greater appreciation and understanding of the value and importance of informal planting."** *The site was originally wooded and many of the large oaks now seen were retained during the clearing of the land. The current collection of fir, spruce, pine, cypress, hemlock, yew and other lesser known conifers is still probably the most extensive to be found on Long Island. Contained within the collection are several trees which, regionally,* *are the largest of their species. Also found are extensive plantings of dwarf evergreens, rhododendron, azaleas, hollies and oaks.*

As we began to tour the land after brunch we passed this huge "thing" planted on the ground. I couldn't tell you what it is called from the outside except that it has leaves...yes it should be a tree. When you walk closer you get to a small opening leading to a walkway inside of what it really is –a HUGE PLANTED TREE! It is gorgeous. It's roots are so deep. It has grown so much that it dug thick branches back into the ground. There are fallen leaves around it so that it is hidden. You can't see the tree because of what has happened over time. It shaped into something peculiar and very distinct.

I ran in first with my camera because I had been there just one month prior. I was truly enjoying each of their faces as they lit up with amazement as they walked inside. I took photos of each woman. I knew they were going to love this! Rightly so! It is something so overwhelming to the eye to take in at once. We spent a long part of our tour time just under this tree. We took so many pictures, climbed, laughed and explored the grounds around this tree. Every one of them loved it, including myself seeing this for the second time.

I bring emphasis to the tree—even the most unusual ones. I am fascinated by them because we are so much like them.

There are times that we don't give things a chance …or an opportunity to reach its full potential. Just as the word of God tells us…as humans we look at the outward appearance but that is not what God is looking at when He sees us. He looks at the core of us. He looks at the inmost place. He looks at the heart. The part that we cover up so well for fear of being exposed and naked before others. When we are vulnerable, we almost expect to get hurt so we put up that covering and wall of protection. Is it such a fear to be exposed? If we are on display… Why? God has it all. What more can we keep from Him. What is there to hide when He sees it all anyway?

Exposed is left or being without shelter or protection; laid open to view; unconcealed; susceptible to attack; vulnerable; to *uncover* or bare to the air; present to view; exhibit or display; to make known, disclose or reveal; unmask; to hold up to public reprehension or ridicule.

Sometimes we even question, what if I can't be ME with YOU? That is probably not good. I want to be me. The flawed me. The natural me. The imperfect me. The growing me. The me that needs help. The me that needs Jesus, that is the me I need to be. He sees me and I trust that SO much. More than any man on earth, for He is my Judge, my Ruler, my Counselor, my everything. And so I brought myself to Him, fully flawed and quickly for I needed rescuing. He saw my heart and wanted to expose just that. And so I surrendered. He saved me. He did the work. There is a covering for me when I am exposed and He places that upon me so that what is reflected internally will outweigh everything I have externally. Just like that tree. There is a beauty inside that He wants to extract.

> ***"O God, You know my foolishness; And my sins are not hidden from You."*** Psalm 69:5 (New King James Version)

> ***"I will abide in Your tabernacle forever; I will trust in the shelter of Your wings. Selah"*** Psalm 61:4 (New King James Version)

> ***"I will put sinews on you and bring flesh upon you, cover you with skin and put breath in you; and you shall live. Then you shall know that I am the Lord."*** Ezekiel 37:6 (New King James Version)

We often think, "but I do want to be me… the uncut version." I want to be me with someone that will accept every part of me. For there is One that will do just that. The Almighty One. The Deliverer. The Savior. The Helper. The Father. The Friend. The One that knows it all ANYWAY. The One that will be with you at all times. You can be your authentic and individual self and allow Him to do that constructive work in you. Give to Him the hidden fully *flawed* part so He can make you fully ***filled*** with His glory. He is looking at that heart of yours. That is what He is waiting for all along. Not based on how you view things but on how He views things in us.

Whatever happened in your life to cover you like this tree, just let it go. Experiences that have altered us in some way over time have made us peculiar too. All these things make us look and act a certain way outwardly. Yet, our focus should not be merely external but the internal which is more valuable in the sight of God and others. So just when you think something may be off and unappealing–it is actually something deep within that makes it real and worthwhile so that you can experience the beauty inside.

GOD SELECTED YOU THIS WAY!

This is a great illustration as we see how King David was selected and singled out among all his family to be the leader of Jerusalem. The part that is worth recognizing, is that no one in the natural would choose this youngster feeding sheep! NO ONE–not even the prophet. And not even his own family! Rejection in the works…imagine a father that has to be asked, "Are you sure there are no other sons???"

"Oh yeah—I remember now, can you guys go get little David from the sheep tending!"

This was simply God orchestrating the moment to select his chosen vessel for the kingdom—the youngest one of all. The forgotten one. And for you my friend, God can select you too. Just like that. He will take you, anoint you, build you and put you on display.

God is always the one in the selection business, not in the way that man would be. For in the eyes of man, we will never be the value that we are to God.

This is a serious story. It is intimate. It is on the life of a loner. The life of the one that is on the back end of things. The one that is last. The one that is young or too old. The one that is inexperienced. The one that messed up. The one that doesn't have much going on. The one that has been through the mud. Yes, if that is you–then you will be the precise one that God will select THEN single out.

You see people are looking for the most qualified to take on a position. They are looking for credentials. They are looking for the degree, certificates, trophies and star badges that you have received. All those things first on the external. Yet God is looking for NONE of that. For He is simply looking for the one that will lead the people back to Him. He is looking for the one that will worship Him in spirit and in truth. He is looking for the one that will inquire of Him. He is looking for the one that will be obedient and say YES to God –even when it doesn't make sense!!!

Using the full detail in 1 Samuel 16:1-13, young David was selected among 7 others. Even in that he was the outlier. For seven is the number of great significance. It represents divine perfection, totality or completion. So in this divine perfection of God, He takes the outlier and makes His presence known! He provides calling and direction to that one that was not a part of that totality. You would think God is doing things out of order. Samuel questioned himself, God and the father of the boys. He said, **"ARE YOU SURE**, that all the men are here!" For to Samuel and Jesse the father, this looked like a great batch of men that could be the next in line for King over Jerusalem...God said, "NOPE–this is not the one!"

> *Then he consecrated Jesse and his sons, and invited them to the sacrifice. So it was, when they came, that he looked at Eliab and said, "Surely the Lord's anointed is before Him!"* **But the Lord said to Samuel, "Do not look at his appearance or at his physical stature, because I have refused him. For the Lord does not see as man sees; for man looks at the outward appearance, but the Lord looks at the heart."** *So Jesse called Abinadab, and made him pass before Samuel. And he said, "Neither has the Lord chosen this one." Then Jesse made Shammah pass by. And he said, "Neither has the Lord chosen this one." Thus Jesse made seven of his sons pass before Samuel. And Samuel said to Jesse, "The Lord has not chosen these." And Samuel said to Jesse, "Are all the young men here?" Then he said, "There* **remains yet the youngest,** *and there he is, keeping the sheep." And Samuel said to Jesse, "Send and bring him. For we will not sit down till he comes here." So he sent and brought him in. Now he was ruddy, with bright eyes, and good-looking. And the Lord said, "Arise, anoint him; for* **this is the one!"** *Then Samuel took the horn of oil and anointed him in the midst of his brothers; and the Spirit of the Lord came upon David from that day forward. So Samuel arose and went to Ramah.* 1 Samuel 16:5-13 (New King James Version)

After Samuel passed through all 7 men, God revealed the last. He made the last first. He made the worst best. He made the runt arise. And he did it in the presence of the rest. That they would recognize and see. God was demonstrating to them all, "The one that you have left out, I have remembered. The one that you ignored, is the one that I was watching. The one that you put to shame, is the one that I have honored. The one that you have disapproved of, is the one that I have approved. The one that you refuse is the one that I will use!"

And to God be the Glory! For indeed He has used the life of many that have fit into this category. The ones with backgrounds similar to this. Samuel was not a bad person. Samuel just needed to see through the eyes of God and not by what he saw as fit. And this is what we need to do at all times. We need to ask God to allow us to see what HE sees. To give us sight for those that have been neglected. To give us a heart for those that are in need. Usually these are the worst types of individuals. But in this God shows us, watch how I take this person from GLORY to GLORY. If I did it with, "Samuel the boy" what makes you think I cannot do it with others. I will take that BOY and make him a MAN of God. I will make him a King. I will make him a man of valor and integrity and this you will see by the heart…and not by any other outward appearance.

God will bring that one that was out in the back end of life into the front line of leadership. He does what is best, what is choice and what will get the job done for real. It takes a pure heart to lead a nation back to the heart of God and that is what King David did when he reigned in Jerusalem. That is what brought God glory…everything else never interrupted the ultimate plan of God. Before David would hit the throne, he knew how to function as a king in the unknown.

God selected David and then singled him out in front of everyone. The glory will come out of the ones with the worst kind of story. That is what salvation is all about. That is the heart of God. That is the will of God. That is the plan that God has for us. He is pulling those inner gifts out. He is extracting things from you that you would never think possible as good. He is so centered on the beauty of your heart—especially when you yield to the calling and purpose.

These writings are to bring healing, encouragement and restoration to your situation. When we look through rose colored glasses at our circumstances, we don't allow the good things to radiate. Restoration is growth. We are all growing. We all have some sort of struggle to get to experience success. But even in falls and stalls, we learn to do things a better way and correctly.

So don't ever think you are not good enough – if God chose you, that is more than ENOUGH!

PIECE 15

MATTERS OF THE HEART

Sometimes we make mistakes, not sure what else to do…especially when it comes to relationships. Many women struggle in this area. They have been hurt by men…even starting from the first one that was supposed to be the primary example. They remain in a constant state of pain because they still love what they lost. They love who left them and they love who lowered their self-worth.

We go all in with our heart…only to break it. Then everything dies…our hope, faith, trust and most importantly, our LOVE for anything else!

We don't know how to respond, so we close up.

One thing I know is that there are good men of God out there. As a married woman of God at the age of 40 I may not have had all the experience in the world but I can share some things with you…HE EXISTS!

You don't need to be abused any longer.

You don't need to be abandoned any longer.
You don't need to be betrayed any longer.
You don't need to be devalued or talked down to any longer.
You don't need to be deceived any longer.
You don't need to be hurt any longer.
You don't need to be used any longer.

You don't need to be disrespected in any way, shape or form any longer!

TRUST GOD… NOT YOUR HEART… and wait. For He will bring the right one to you.

I had such an amazing and liberating discussion recently. It is like all my life I wanted someone else to say it, then the words spilled out.

"I walked down the aisle a SECOND time and still UNSURE. When I finally realized that this wasn't about the love we think of. My first time I married because I loved him! This time I married because HE LOVED ME and that was worth it. It is not about me loving but about HIM loving me. That is how I knew it was going to be a good life for me. That I would LEARN TO LOVE this man that God gave me." Wow—still in awe reading this powerful and honest statement.

This is a lasting love. The one that is learned and practiced, not the one that is "felt". It is not about the butterflies in the tummy or the one that makes you blush, but it is about the one who will RESPECT YOU!

HE WILL HONOR YOU!
HE WILL EXALT YOU!

HE WILL PROVIDE FOR YOU!
HE WILL TAKE SPECIAL CARE FOR YOU!
HE WILL CATER TO YOUR NEEDS!
HE WILL ENJOY YOU… YES, JUST YOU!
HE WILL BUILD YOU UP!
HE WILL MOTIVATE YOU IN A GOOD WAY!
HE WILL APPRECIATE EVERYTHING ABOUT YOU!
HE WILL BE PATIENT WITH YOU!
HE WILL SUPPORT YOU IN EVERY WHICH WAY!
HE WILL BRING THE BEST OUT OF YOU!

That is the one that you need! Not the one by feelings…for all that comes and goes!

But the one that does all of that…is THE one from God, for he is only fulfilling the scriptures.

And here he goes, outlined like this…

> *"Husbands, go all out in your love for your wives, exactly as Christ did for the church—a love marked by giving, not getting. Christ's love makes the church whole. His words evoke her beauty. Everything he does and says is designed to bring the best out of her, dressing her in dazzling white silk, radiant with holiness. And that is how husbands ought to love their wives. They're really doing themselves a favor—since they're already "one" in marriage. No one abuses his own body, does he? No, he feeds and pampers it. That's how Christ treats us, the church, since we are part of his body. And this is why a man leaves father and mother and*

> *cherishes his wife. No longer two, they become "one flesh." This is a huge mystery, and I don't pretend to understand it all. What is clearest to me is the way Christ treats the church. And this provides a good picture of how each husband is to treat his wife, loving himself in loving her, and how each wife is to honor her husband."* Ephesians 5:25-33 (The Message)

I can share with you that there is a man that went all out of his way for me on earth. That is the one that placed this ring on my finger. He demonstrated a Christ-like love for me and I appreciate that in every way. Hearing so many horror stories and even been through some myself. I can say that I have a man of God in my life. I am thankful. For even when you may not have been the best–he was still the best in his way and the best for me.

Isn't that exactly how it is written in Ephesians 5 above? I would say surely it is. Husbands must love their wives just as Christ loves the church. He showed me one that would do his utmost to love me in an unconditional way.

Honestly we don't have that fairy tale type of situation but it is our own unique agape love story that has kept us this long. My husband when he first met me – got a wreck literally! But he pursued me for whatever crazy reason that was. I would have to say 150% that was it was a God thing. Because I didn't have an easy upbringing he got me right in chaos.

I grew up in the Bronx in a house on the corner by a train station. I remember brief details but do recall the most significant being the day that my mom left my father. She had enough and decided to create a new life without him. It was dark out and I remember asking her, "Where are we going?" She said, "To our new home." I just didn't know that our new home was going to be so broken. It was incomplete and she was going to have to do it all by herself. She was upset, yet strong to muster up the courage to lead us to this place. It was me on one hand about 6 years old and my brother on the other about 8 years old. From that point forward I would say that my mom struggled every day without even admitting that to us, but it was felt in our upbringing. She turned to a life of hard work, some party living, reliance on government assistance until she was not able to work due to a rising ailment.

I think I always was missing something in my life because of our home situation. There was an absence of a man. A father-figure or a supposed love that would protect and cover me. I really didn't know what to do with my life and I never really made the best decisions when it came to personal aspects because of having this void in my life that was never really explained accurately. I didn't know what relationships were about or how they should look. We lived beside my aunt, uncle and cousins and that was the only snap shot that I could see but that didn't really get me an inside scoop as it relates to marriage and intimacy. I was completely clueless even as I gave my virginity away at the age of 14 for no reason at all. I met a young kid once in the night. The next time we meet we had intercourse. The next day I called him and he tells me not to call him. That was the day I think I realized how much of a fool I was at understanding relationships. As the tears stung my eyes and I hung up the phone I made a mental "note to self" never to give my heart completely to any man because I would need to protect that only piece of me. How could something important end up being so meaningless to some still boggles me.

At 16 I had extracted a sexually transmitted disease from another one-off incident, yet it was something. At 17, I met the man who is now my husband and have been with him ever since. We have 2 children 8 years apart. Unfortunately, due to my lack of understanding and relationship skills, I would ultimately end up repeatedly hurting my husband, my children and even myself due to choices that I thought were best to fill this unquenchable void and absence in my life. I would say that I needed a lot of rearing in the techniques of marriage, parenting, leadership and education. I still find myself to be in a humble state of learning day by day because these pieces of my life are never-ending and should always yield good fruit.

At 22, I had given my life over to Jesus Christ through a simple prayer of salvation. This was the first time that I invited Jesus into my life and received a new beginning and chance at life. I then officially married my husband 2 years later, to be exact. I immediately came into a committed life "full throttle" but realized I was going to hit many speed bumps during this journey. There were just so many things stemming from my childhood that created me to be the way that I was and I needed a lot of fixing. I suffered severe depression, suicidal thoughts, drunkenness, anger, rage, multiple addictions and every other thing that would temporarily bring me comfort in order to fill a deep void that was present in my life even after having invited Jesus into my life.

Did you know that even in marriage you could suffer with loneliness? In a crowded room filled with family and friends you could feel deserted. With all these pressing situations I made so many mistakes. I could not even count all of them in my initial process trying to live the life as a Christian. Everything was difficult for me and to battle each issue (for there were many) individually was like moving Mount Everest!

Throughout my life, without realizing, I had allowed some person or another to have a soul tie with. Since there was a wound that was caused, it left an area of vulnerability for the enemy to come in and have a field day with my life! I would not realize until today how much of a great struggle and suffering that I would be living through as the enemy has done all that he has to lure me into the same type of lifestyle common to my parents. Most people can't admit that and constantly have some struggle, emotionally, sexually, physically, spiritually, but as for me in every aspect of this – I fell short. Not only did I fall but it was a masterpiece of a mess!

That moment from the Identity Retreat in Florida, I spoke with God so deeply after repeated breaking over my soul. I had surrendered my life back to God realizing that my life was never going to be my own. My life was never going to be manageable until I surrendered it into the hands of the One that would forever protect and cover me completely! I stood on that lake realizing through the many trials that I have been through and have even caused myself that He kept me alive. I have survived! I just knew that this word must reign in my life all of my days. I had to receive God completely. I took the gift [of grace] that I kept on rejecting and I never want to go back to that lifestyle.

> *"I will lift up my eyes to the hills from whence comes my help? My help comes from the Lord, who made heaven and earth. He will not allow your foot to be moved; He who keeps you will not slumber. Behold, He who Keeps Israel shall neither slumber nor sleep. The Lord is your keeper; The Lord is your shade at your right hand. The sun shall not strike you by day, nor the moon by night. The Lord shall preserve you from all evil; He shall preserve your soul. The Lord shall preserve your going out and your coming in from this time forth, and even forevermore.* Psalm 121 (New King James Version)

With this, I have seen restoration in my home. It is different. It has been saved. We are in a restoration process and it is beautiful. My husband and I are constantly working to renew, restore and rebuild. We place our flawed relationship before our King. He places His covering over it and seals us. I love the way he has embraced me in every way. It is not all sun, roses and rainbows but it is BETTER and it is as REAL as it is going to get.

In being honest with each other –hurtful or not we lay all our cards on the table. Some are just so difficult. But we get through it and we tell each other, "This is really not easy, but let's try again." And we keep fighting. We trust God.

My relationship with my children has changed in a whole 360! We are very close as it stands today. Very open with each other. The good, the bad, the ugly—that's all for God to settle and seal it. We talk. We share. We laugh. We cry. We are a real family that was broken and has now been restored. God is doing that and so are we. We are putting in the effort. We saw where **we** fell short and are working to make changes and make it better. There is grace over us. Love over us. Peace over us. We will all stand together despite what we have to face, there is more grace.

There is His love poured out. God is pouring Himself over this situation.

God is love. God demonstrated that to us. In that, while we were still sinners, He died for the ungodly [Romans 5:6]. I may be repetitive in some of my writings only because these are the words and scriptures that I hold so near and dear to myself. I hang onto those powerful words! Because no matter what I have done or what we have done–HE STILL LOVES US! That is the gift!!!

If you are still waiting, enjoy the wait because it takes a lot of work to cultivate the family. God hasn't forgotten you. He has that all in place for you and what you need exists. Christ is that first man and will be the one also to lead you to the man like this! Don't ever stop believing. It is not based on a feeling but based on the actions of character and integrity that are all outlined throughout the scriptures. The same way I still had to go to the first Man – called the Son of God is the same way we all need to go through too. This whole journey is to create a connection with our Main Man

[Jesus] so that if any piece of us experiences something less, we go to the One with more.

If you don't feel appreciated or celebrated enough as you are reading now—I tell you congratulations on your recovery! Look at how far you have come! Look how far God can take you. Your reward is going to be so amazing. Because you are a rare breed indeed. You have been set apart and are uniquely designed for something greater.

During our process we have to make those certain pit stops and learn to celebrate how far we have come in life. Not everything is such a complete wreck. That is how Jesus looks at you. With love and with awe. He is so mindful of you. You are always on His mind.

> *What is mankind that You are mindful of them, human beings that You care for them? You have made them a little lower than the angels and crowned them with glory and honor. You made them rulers over the works of your hands; You put everything under their feet: All flocks and herds, and the animals of the wild, The birds in the sky, and the fish in the sea, All that swim the paths of the seas. Lord, our Lord, How majestic is your name in all the earth!* Psalm 8:4-9 (New International Version)

The angels asked God, "Why are you so mindful of them?" In other words, they were saying, "Here we are as bright shining angels and you are not taking note of us like those on earth." But God is so in love with you that is carefully paying attention to your every move.

When we don't receive this love and acceptance from Him all we are doing is rejecting the gift that He has given to us. Don't reject the love that He has for you and what He has done for you. He has given you His best and freed you from a life of mess.

We are free. It is finished –He has done it! That redemptive work is done!

> ***Where, O death, is your victory? Where, O death, is your sting? The sting of death is sin, and the power of sin is the law. But thanks be to God! He gives us victory through our Lord Jesus Christ.*** 1 Corinthians 15:55-56 (New International Version)

Just because you felt rejected or experienced disappointment doesn't mean you have to lash out that way. We don't need to reject the one thing that was given to us as the best gift of all. Go to God with arms wide open, with a grateful heart and with hope for your future receiving that gift.

Stop rejecting the gift of love, grace, redemption, mercy, renewal and restoration. Receive a new life, a new walk, a new focus and an established purpose. You are here today and should recognize how important you are. Your very life matters! That is why God wanted you to know that—even when you were at the worst of your worst. When you were at the lowliest state. When you felt defeated. When you felt lost. When you felt like there was no way out of your mess. God gave the best for you to be restored.

REBUILT: Beginning the Ending

PIECE 16

MAKE FREQUENT STOPS AND REST

TRUCK MAKES FREQUENT STOPS

I was driving behind this truck with a good friend in my car and took a moment to snap this photo. I said, "This will be a great title for my next blog!" If I have to have patience to drive behind this big truck blocking my beautiful view that could be quite frustrating. Then I quickly thought, "If the truck needs to make frequent stops, shouldn't we?" Certainly we should. For even the Word declares in Genesis 2:1-2, "Thus the heavens and the earth were completed in all their vast array. By the seventh day God had finished the work He had been doing; so on the seventh day He rested from all His work." If God took the seventh day to rest in the beginning of time, that is probably a good indicator that it is also necessary for us as humans to stop frequently and take a rest as well.

We get so busy in life with full-time jobs, relationships, parenting, social networking, exercising, and so many more activities. Even as Christians we need to take time daily for prayer, regular worship, study of the bible, church attendance, activities and fellowship. This kind of consistent business, even though it is good for us, requires us to rest. Sometimes it may even mean that we don't answer the frequent phone calls, text messages and perhaps even a disconnect from social media so that we give our minds and hearts a break from life. Is that a bad thing to just take a moment and stop engaging yourself in every activity under the sun? No it is not. As much as all these things are good for us it is also necessary for us to rest from it all. If any of those things are true to us, then they will still be there when we return from our rest. It doesn't mean we are isolating ourselves or separating forever. It simply means we are going to make a decision to make frequent stops so that we can actually function more effectively.

To stop means to cease from, to interrupt, to discontinue, restrain and prevent from proceeding or operating. Imagine how much better we will function if we make frequent stops at everything that we do. If we work

Monday through Friday 9-5, then it should stop at 5 and the same goes for weekends. We can make ourselves over obligated and committed to every task that comes our way. What happens if we don't do it? IT CAN WAIT! Your health is the priority. Your mind is the priority and the soundness of that mind. The bible says in Ecclesiastes 8:5, "Whoever obeys his command will come to no harm, and the wise heart will know the **proper time** and procedure. For there is a **proper time** and procedure for **every matter**, though a man's misery weighs heavily upon him."

There are so many other bible references that help us in this area:

> 1 Corinthians 10:23, "Everything is permissible but **not everything is beneficial**. Everything is permissible but **not everything is constructive**."

> Ecclesiastes 3:1, "There is a **time for everything** [includes rest] and a season for every activity under heaven."

> Ecclesiastes 12:12, "Be warned, my son of anything in addition to them. Of making many books there is no end, and **much study wearies the body**."

> 1 John 2:19, "This then is how we know that we belong to the truth and how we set our hearts at **rest in His presence**."

> Matthew 11:20, "Come to Me, all you who are **weary** [physically or mentally exhausted by hardwork, exertion, strain, etc.; fatigued; tired] and **burdened**

[loaded, borne with difficulty; to load oppressively] and **I will give you rest.**"

I had to stop at that scripture in Matthew 11...

I have come to a point where I allowed myself to become overwhelmed. Too many things beginning to weigh me down at once. I was even thinking, "Who can I trust?" Not one person really, when everyone does this or that. It is so hard especially when I am going through my darkest hour. I think I didn't even want to go to God that is how overwhelmed I was. I didn't know what else to say to Him but the same thing over and over again. I felt like I was being so repetitious, even in my tears. What else could I really do here? I try to stay as strong as I can but how strong is that really? I read my life in a book by Holley Gerth, "What Your Heart Needs for the Hard Days."

"Through disappointments, circumstances not going as we planned; putting our trust in imperfect people that let us down; where nothing turns out as we expected; our heads and what happens just don't align or match. He says "Come here. Lean on Me. Put the full weight of your need on ME. I can handle it. I love you and I will not let you down."

I need rest – the refreshing quiet or repose of sleep; refreshing ease or inactivity after exertion or labor; relief or freedom, especially from anything that wearies, troubles or disturbs. Quite honestly at times, my life can be very disturbing, my mind can be disturbing, people at work can be disturbing, church folks can be disturbing, family can even get exhausting and disturbing too. That is real talk. That is life. I just need some rest. I went through too many times trying to function when I feel dysfunctional and I have to stop that! I am tired. If you want to be **restored,** then you have to make sure that you *take the time to rest.*

Rest is good and rest helps me. It gives me strength – God gives it to me. I need to receive it and not reject or fight against what He is begging to give me. Even when I make too many plans, He cancels them time and time again. God has a different agenda for my life, to remove what I do and replace it with what He does. He wants me to be overwhelmed with His peace and not with weariness.

I came up from prayer and heard Him whisper to me, "Your healing is here, your freedom is here, when you rest. Yes, when you REST in My presence!" Just like the song by Deluge, "Healing is Here." The bridge of the song proclaims:

Sickness can't stay any longer
Your perfect love is casting out fear
You are the God of All Power
and it is Your will that my life be healed

That is a truth for us all. It is the will of God for my life to be healed. Healing is here, right in the very presence of God. Don't allow yourself to become this burdened. As large as responsibilities are and just like the truck in the picture here carrying a lot of products, that requires frequent stops until the load gets lighter to run more efficiently. Take the time to rest. Drop the load off. Do something that you enjoy. Close your eyes and get some rest. Shut off your cell phone, put up a "do not disturb" sign and gets some guilt-free rest! The same way God wants you whole and healthy is the same way others will benefit more from a stabilized and controlled version of you, rather than one that is stressed out to full capacity and ready to blow up.

Give yourself permission to rest. You don't need permission from someone else to take a break. God grants it to you through His Word and through His presence. Trust and receive that gift from God. Create a new rule for yourself that says, "I am not just going to rest when I am beyond exhausted but I am going to make it my new obligation to **MAKE FREQUENT STOPS** so that I can be more effective in everything else that I do."

PIECE 17
ATTITUDE IS EVERYTHING

HUMILITY DEFINED…. In restoration we have to develop an attitude of humility. That is a must. It is a COMPLETE submission, surrender and a sacrifice to not be the one that needs stuff done their own way. It is doing more for others. Fix self, so you are good around others. Everyone will benefit from. You can't remain bitter, angry, dry, disconnected, defensive, frustrated, stubborn or the like. Humility will win in your situation every single time.

> *Your attitude should be the same as that of Christ Jesus: who, being in the very nature of God, did not consider equality with God something to be grasped, but made Himself nothing taking the very nature of a servant, being made in human likeness. And being found in appearance as a man, He humbled Himself and became obedient to death- even death on a cross!* Philippians 2:5-8 (New International Version)

This is a true humility [a modest view of one's own importance; the act or posture of lowering oneself in relation to others, or conversely, having a clear perspective and respect for one's place in context]. The humility that we learn as believers in Christ. For if Jesus Himself took off His Royalty, was sent down in human (flawed) form, and endured all suffering– all the way to the point of death then how much more shall we practice this same principle. The bible declares in Matthew 23:12, "For whoever exalts himself will be humbled and whoever humbles himself will be exalted!"

Jesus had a clear perspective. He had us in mind. He was not considering His own importance of being but considered the importance of us! Jesus had no issue with humility. He was humility defined. For us, we must adhere to this character. That's all that it takes to win the war within, at home, at work, at church and in every place. The enemy is trying to rob us of precious time! We MUST seek God in this and bring any stubborn and resistant behavior into subjection. How? Through prayer! Lots of prayer! Fervent prayer! By constant prayer! David grasped this concept by practicing a life of worship and prayer. For many kings in their exalted role would struggle in this area. For David wrote in Psalm 35:13-34, "Yet when they were ill, I put on sackcloth and humbled myself with fasting. When my prayers returned to me unanswered, I went about mourning as though for my friend or brother. I bowed my head in grief as though weeping for my mother."

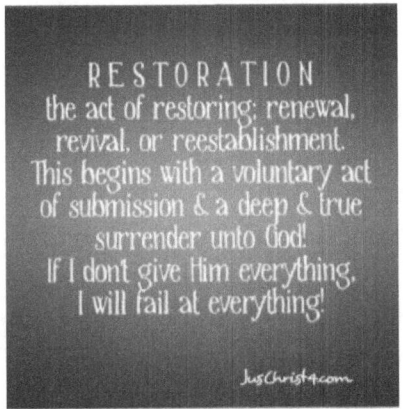

Other kings in the word are outlined all through 1 and 2 Kings after David and Solomon. They were humbled. For those that surrendered and submitted wholeheartedly to God were prosperous and protected! King Nebuchadnezzar was humbled in Daniel 4:28-34. He was brought to a humbling experience, then he received an exchange of restoration.

God wants us to be humble too. We have to give God access to every area in our life so that He can govern it! If we don't acknowledge Him or invite Him in, then how can we expect Him to intervene on our behalf? We have to allow Him access to ABIDE! Abide is to remain!!! For this is what humility and submission is all about.

Jesus said in John 15:1-7, "I am the true vine, and my Father is the gardener. He cuts off every branch in me that bears no fruit, while every branch that does bear fruit he prunes so that it will be even more fruitful. You are already clean because of the word I have spoken to you. Remain in me, as I also remain in you. No branch can bear fruit by itself; it must remain in the vine. Neither can you bear fruit unless you remain in me. "I am the vine; you are the branches. If you remain in me and I in you, you will bear much fruit; apart from me you can do nothing. If you do not remain in me, you are like a branch that is thrown away and withers; such branches are picked up, thrown into the fire and burned. If you remain in me and my words remain in you, ask whatever you wish, and it will be done for you."

If we do not abide in Him, we won't be able to do anything on our own strength! Nothing will last. Nothing will survive. Nothing will bear fruit the way that God intends for our life. He wants us to experience MUCH fruit. Not for us to be hanging on by a limb! But for every place in our life to yield forth fruit! This is how we will gain the victory. And it takes being humble.

Humility defined is simply this…Jesus Christ giving up all so that we can have it all. A life of abundance. So if He humbled Himself, then certainly we must. We can't go on living through this war-zone of a life thinking that we have it all covered just by our own stubborn ways. It is time to give God the dominion. It is time for us to believe that we can have this abundant life when we learn how to function through humble acts. Especially for our home, our marriage, our children, our career, our finances, our health and so much more. It is not worth fighting for all this on our own strength when there is a way that shows us better.

The Son of Man showed us that way. Jesus gave humility a definition. He is the ultimate example and sacrifice. If you are tired of fighting so hard, let the guards down. Humble yourself in the sight of God and He will lift you up [James 4:10]. His word [Christ Jesus] is living proof and a guarantee of that.

REBUILT: Beginning the Ending

PIECE 18

POWERFUL PRAYERS

Powerful prayers can be in many forms. In order to experience a full restoration our prayer life needs to be restored as well. We find a way to talk back and reach the heart of God. It is not always about how loud you pray or how eloquent the words are—in the end it is simply having a conversation with God and spending time in His presence. Sometimes in conversation we are excited, sad, with fewer words or with many. It really all ranges on the moment. In any case, THEY ALL WORK! Just pray because He hears it all and just wants us to spend that precious quality time with Him. Talk to God... YES! About anything and everything.

> *"Devote yourselves to prayer, being watchful and thankful."* Colossians 4:2 NIV

> *"Be joyful in hope, patient in affliction, faithful in prayer."* Romans 12:12 NIV

We need to be devoted to prayer. We need to be faithful in prayer. We need to be consistent in prayer. "Pray without ceasing." 1 Thessalonians 5:17

This reminds us not to give up. Never to quit. To travail and make our prayers ardent. Corrie Ten Boom stated, "Is prayer your steering wheel or is it your spare tire?" Do we talk to someone and only reach out when we have a problem? That should never be the case when it comes to matters of the heart or with people that you care for. With that being said, God should be the utmost for your list of favorite people to converse with. Just ask Him, "Hear my cry, O God; listen to my prayer." Psalm 61:1

Powerful things happen when we pray too! Prayer changes things. Prayer moves mountains in our lives. The same way the apostles prayed often in the book of Acts. They saw God move on their behalf. Look at what prayer does for us.

Fills us with the Holy Spirit

> ***"And when they had prayed, the place where they were assembled together was shaken; and they were all filled with the Holy Spirit, and they spoke the word of God with boldness."*** Acts 4:31 (New King James Version)

Makes us believe

> ***"So when they had appointed elders in every church, and prayed with fasting, they commended them to the Lord in whom they had believed."*** Acts 14:23

Gives us deliverance

> "And David built there an altar to the Lord, and offered burnt offerings and peace offerings. So the Lord heeded the prayers for the land, and the plague was withdrawn from Israel." 2 Samuel 24:25

> "Peter was therefore kept in prison, but constant prayer was offered to God for him by the church. And when Herod was about to bring him out, that night Peter was sleeping, bound with two chains between two soldiers; and the guards before the door were keeping the prison. Now behold, an angel of the Lord stood by him, and a light shone in the prison; and he struck Peter on the side and raised him up, saying, "Arise quickly!" And his chains fell off his hands. Then the angel said to him, "Gird yourself and tie on your sandals"; and so he did. And he said to him, "Put on your garment and follow me." So he went out and followed him, and did not know that what was done by the angel was real, but thought he was seeing a vision. When they were past the first and the second guard posts, they came to the iron gate that leads to the city, which opened to them of its own accord; and they went out and went down one street, and immediately the angel departed from him. And when Peter had come to himself, he said, "Now I know for certain that the Lord has sent His angel, and has delivered me from the hand of Herod and from all the expectation of the Jewish people." Acts 12:5-14

> "Who, in the days of His flesh, when He had offered up

> *prayers and supplications, with vehement cries and tears to Him who was able to save Him from death, and was heard because of His godly fear…"* Hebrews 5:7

Brings us healing

> *"So Abraham prayed to God; and God healed Abimelech, his wife, and his female servants. Then they bore children; for the Lord had closed up all the wombs of the house of Abimelech because of Sarah, Abraham's wife"* Genesis 20:17-18

Gives us peace

> *"And seek the peace of the city where I have caused you to be carried away captive, and pray to the Lord for it; for in its peace you will have peace."* Jeremiah 29:7 (New King James Version)

No matter what the need is during that very moment, it could be a difficult situation or it could just be a time of rest. As we talk to God, we can be assured that He will be responding on our behalf. And never feel like you are not good enough or holy enough for prayer. For all these things Christ has done [Ephesians 2:13] so that we can draw near to God and He will draw near to us [James 4:8]. It doesn't matter the form either–there is no protocol but action! Men and women in the bible knelt, laid prostrate, cried, stood, sat and even whispered during their prayer times. God heard them all. The same way He hears you! Now that makes such a ***powerful prayer*** indeed. This brings us to His presence so that you learn who He is.

I don't understand how people can be non-responsive through prayer and in the very presence of the Lord.

As for me, there are so many times that I just want to fall down, cry, scream, shout, yell, sing, run, dance, preach and sometimes even laugh for the joy inexpressible.

There is nothing better for me than being in the atmosphere of the Lord. He is everywhere. He is present at all times.

I am there in the midst of a powerful worship service and I can feel Him reading my heart like no other. He is whispering things to me. Good things. Favorable things.

> *"When the Son of Man comes in His glory, and all the angels with Him, He will sit on His glorious throne. All the nations will be gathered before Him, and He will separate the people one from another as a shepherd separates the sheep from the goats. He will put the sheep on His right and the goats on His left. Then the King will say to those on His right, 'Come, you who are blessed by my Father; take your inheritance, the kingdom prepared for you since the creation of the world. For I was hungry and you gave me something to eat, I was thirsty and you gave me something to drink, I was a stranger and you invited me in, I needed clothes and you clothed me, I was sick and you looked after me, I was in prison and you came to visit me.'"* Matthew 25:31-36 (New International Version)

This verse speaks to how the human relationship is with

serving others but we can also see how Jesus used Himself first as an example to describe our service to Him as well. When do we make that time for God? When do we invite Him in our lives or visit Him intimately through a separated time of devotion. I can be in the midst of such amazing and strong atmospheres of worship and feel a manifested presence of God. I immediately react. I respond. If I just sat there, I listen or I silently pray. I am always doing something to reflect upon the beauty of His holiness...

> **"Give unto the Lord the glory due to His name; Worship the Lord in the beauty of holiness."** Psalm 29:2 (New King James Version)

It is a gift to be able to worship the Lord. To be able to express our love and emotions.

To express our thoughts. To express all our anguish or frustration. To give to God all that we are experiencing and stand up feeling whole. There is nothing more glorious than being in His midst. It is unforgettable. It is undeniable. It is incomparable. It is inexpressible. What could be as fascinating as His nearness, His closeness, and His tangible presence in our lives? Nothing else matters at that moment. It is just you and a God that is matchless. A God that is able to fill you up beyond capacity. So that you are overflowing with His love.

There is something so profound and powerful that occurs when we worship our God. I surrender everything to Him at that moment. I say "Yes" again. For whatever He wants me to do. For whatever He requires of me. I say it all over again until I am completely emptied of everything that tries to resist or hinder this relationship that I have with the King. All other worries flee. Thoughts become clear and concise. New strength is obtained in these moments. A fresh peace washes over my soul. I stand content. I am able to move forward. I can breathe again.

I don't care who is around me. I don't care who is watching me. I don't care about any problems. I don't stop myself from giving my all to Him because He is in fact the one relationship that matters most. He is the King of kings and the Lord of lords. To worship our Lord in the midst of mess is the most liberating experience when you give your all.

REBUILT: Beginning the Ending

PIECE 19

PUSH PAST PAIN

PUSH PAST PAIN – KEEP PUSHING; THE ONLY WAY TO GET PAST IS TO GO THROUGH IT

John 16:33, "These things I have spoken to you, that in Me you may have peace. In the world you will have tribulation [grievous trouble; severe trial or suffering]; but be of good cheer, I have overcome the world."

At first I hurt myself, then I kept going. 18 stations in total and I felt pain at the first one. At each station you will have 50 seconds of work and 30 seconds of rest before switching to the next. Warm up was hard. I felt like my heart was beating out of my chest. It hurt but I kept on running behind the rest. I stood at my own pace, I didn't try to outrun anyone. I met the trainer at the stop and he gave us all a high five as we went in to the rooms to then start the intense cardio. Clearly I could see this was not going to be an easy session. At the stations were dips, toe touch sit-ups then a repeat of this three times. Hop squats were next, then back to arms by doing curls and pulls for triceps; sit up twists, a repeat of hop squats, high knee jumps, push-ups, and more bar curls. There are about 20 other people in the room. Some more fit then the others but each have a different shape, pace and response to the intense workout routine. We motivate each other and we focus. We also have moments of complete anguish while going through each of the stations. It hurts and it doesn't get any easier at the next station.

While I was at the station for dips on triceps, since it has been a while I felt a huge pull. I only did about 3 to 4 reps of dips. I felt like I pulled my muscle badly. I let out a sound of sharp pain. I tried to continue but this really hurt and it was hindering me from completing the 50 seconds just at this station. This is because my own workout routine significantly declined over the last several months. I slowed down my pace and have not been as diligent for working out as I was. I always worked out my arms, legs and did other cardio routines. My stamina was a lot better before and you could see that my body was taking on a good shape and definition. Then I slacked off. Tonight I was paying for it in this room during such an intensified workout routine. I knew I did it before –why so much pain then, "UGH!"

The funny thing was that after I hurt myself at the dip station, I just paused and picked up another pace at the next. Then I started banging them out like nothing. Even the people near me were like "You keep going!" The trainer was even proud of me. He said I really brought it with my effort. I was surprised at how continuing through the stations made me push past the pain. Despite being hurt, I

Push Past Pain

just kept going. I completed the 18 station workout TWICE with the opening warm up. Boot camp session all done. It was finally over. Everybody was dripping and soaking wet like we just got out of a pool. Then comes the water and fresh air. The time of refreshing.

Driving home I thought to myself, "Wow I did it!" As much as I dread the intense workout, the pain from heavy movement, the sick feeling of nausea and the strain on ever part of my body, I was able to complete it. So much more I have to do. I thought about my life now. Everything that has hurt me and tried to destroy me. All the pain I have to endure from LIFE. It is a part of it. We can't escape those things but we can certainly get through it until our time for refreshing comes. The bible tells us, "In this world YOU WILL HAVE TRIBULATION but take heart...I have overcome." So this means that we can do it as well. The bible also tells us in Philippians 4:13 that we can do all things through Christ. We need Him to go through it. We need God to help us push past the pain. When it hurts the most and we come up kicking and screaming –we have to be patient to wait 'til the refreshing comes. Just keep going.

If you are crying... keep going.

If you are hurting... keep going.

If you are stressing... keep going.

If everything looks like it is impossible... just keep going!

No matter what you are experiencing, just keep going. Initially things hurt a whole lot but then as you keep moving forward you will get to the point of rest. Sometimes it will hurt the whole way through but you are not alone. You are not the only one that has to go through the heavy routines and boot camps of life. Your trainer is an EXPERT that is guiding you and others through. Watching you. Coaching you. Cheering you on. He is smiling upon you when He sees you go through and finish the assignment that He planned for you. Trust Him…He is in the best shape ever. We look up to our Trainer. We believe our Trainer. We endure with our Trainer. Our goal is to look like and function just like our Trainer. We can do it. He is WITH us!

"Through God, we will do valiantly." Psalm 60:12

We are going to arrive at that place where we will be in the best shape ever…in every aspect of our lives. Just push past the pain!!!

The storms of life are going to come. It is a part of life. We have our sunny days, rainy days, cold days, hot days, foggy days, windy days and our stormy days! It is a fluctuating cycle! Maybe it is disappointing, maybe it is trying you further, maybe it is not the progress you want to see happen rapidly but we must remember beyond the moment is the mandate. Push for that. Make that your goal. It is our eternal weight of glory that will make the difference.

> *For this light momentary affliction is preparing for us an eternal weight of glory beyond all comparison, as we look not to the things that are seen but to the things that are unseen. For the things that are seen are transient,*

but the things that are unseen are eternal. 2 Corinthians 4:17-18

I was watching the reality show "Blackzilians" and found it so intriguing. It caught my attention because one of the fighters said, "I don't care if I lose 4 out of 5 fights, I just know that the fire is going to come." They had to discuss the reality of loss. He had a very positive perspective on fighting. It doesn't always mean that you celebrate the victories, but that you also learn how to deal with the losses. Don't allow loss to make you quit and throw in the towel. If passion is what drives you, not winning, then you should never quit because of a loss.

There was another guy scheduled to fight and he caught a seizure. The whole team felt the impact of him being down. They had to find someone else in the team to step up and fight. As all the men stood, you see that there were so many. I think what really brings success is having a team of good fighters put together. Of all the men there, each will have a different gift, skill set, talent, speed, coordination, agility and strength. Does that mean that one is less than the other? What it means is that every person on that team has something unique about them in order to fight. This makes each of them valuable in their own way. For when one is not able to fight on that day, someone else can fight for them!

1 Timothy 6:12 tells us, "Fight the good fight of faith, lay hold on eternal life, to which you were also called and have confessed the good confession in the presence of many witnesses." So no matter what we are going through, we

have to keep on fighting our way through it. There are going to be days where you win some and lose some. You are going to have to get your hands dirty. You are going to have to learn to fall. You are going to have to learn to embrace pain. You will have to learn all these things so that you conquer all your fears and failures in order to get back up strong.

Being strong is having, showing, or able to exert great bodily or muscular power; physically vigorous or robust; accompanied or delivered by great physical, mechanical, etc., power or force; mentally powerful or vigorous; especially able, competent, or powerful in a specific field or respect; of great moral power, firmness, or courage.

We cannot quit. We have to get mentally strong. We have to break through our darkest hours in life in order to really appreciate the light that is certain to come. Apostle Paul must have felt that in his darkest hour of imprisonment. Yet he took the time still to encourage others like Timothy, "Fight the good fight!" He was telling him not to give up and not to quit. He was familiar with failure, disappointment, discouragement, battle and turmoil. Why else would he know to write such encouraging words?

> *"Be strong in the Lord and in the power of His might"*
> Ephesians 6:10 (New King James Version)

> *"I know what it is to be in need, and I know what it is to have plenty. I have learned the secret of being content in any and every situation, whether well fed or hungry,*

whether living in plenty or in want." Philippians 4:12 (New International Version)

"That is why, for Christ's sake, I delight in weaknesses, in insults, in hardships, in persecutions, in difficulties. For when I am weak, then I am strong." 2 Corinthians 12:10 (New International Version)

Moments of weakness are going to come but so are the good moments! I have been studying book that has been so helpful for my walk in the Lord, "What Your Heart Needs for the Hard Days" by Holley Gerth. This book has been extremely insightful especially when I feel myself passing through those dark days. We all have them. I shared this with my counselor friend and he said, "Why are you only focused on the hard days? What is your heart going to do on the good days?" I looked at him and I just shook my head because he is always right. I can't just look at the hard days but I have to consider the good days that I have as well.

Looking back at the minds of these men that are professional fighters, I could just relate with the tenacity that they have. They continue no matter what happens. They get wounded, feel loss, and surely feel the pain but they train hard in order to endure all of that. Likewise, we have to train our spirits to be prepared for the fights we will have to encounter as well. Same concept as the soldier that is outlined in its entirety of Ephesians 6. We have an ongoing war and there are ways to win it! Just don't let the bad days take you so far off course. Stay the course. Keep fighting. For your victory is definitely going to happen as well. So gear up, put on your boxing gloves and stand tall!

Even though you win some and lose some, you will be sure to have an amazing comeback if you just don't quit!

PIECE 20
SEASONS OF CHANGE

There is nothing greater when you have come to the point in your walk with God that you see the change. That experience alone to recognize, what God is working in you—is WORKING!!!

The bible records in 4 separate books that we shall love the Lord our God with all our heart, with all our soul, with all our mind and with all our strength! That is every part of your being – fully connected to God. This is an amazing feeling. A liberating experience. This is our freedom not just to say it but to live it!

Makes me feel like a colorful tree planted so deep in the roots of Christ Jesus. I am so filled now and I want more!

> *"You shall love the Lord your God with all your heart, with all your soul, and with all your strength."*
> Deuteronomy 6:5 (New King James Version)

> *Jesus said to him, "You shall love the Lord your God with all your heart, with all your soul, and with all your mind. This is the first and great commandment."*
> Matthew 22:37-38 (New King James Version)

> *"And you shall love the Lord your God with all your heart, with all your soul, with all your mind, and with all your strength. This is the first commandment."*
> Mark 12:30 (New King James Version)

> *"So He answered and said, You shall love the Lord your God with all your heart, with all your soul, with all your strength, and with all your mind, and your neighbor as yourself."* Luke 10:27 (New King James Version)

This is as if each time that it is mentioned it becomes more magnified and detailed. The first commandment is to love God with all of our being. The second commandment is to love others just as we would ourselves. Which fulfills the law, because Christ died for all. He gave His life so that we can have our life. In that same way we would be able to have an experience and a concept of an agape [unconditional] type of love.

For just as my progression has moved passed the year, I rejoice at the change. I rejoice when people tell me that I am different from the year before. I rejoice when I sense my spirit prompting me from right and wrong. I rejoice when I hear God's word running through my mind to cancel out the bad thoughts. I rejoice when my heart feels pure and experiences new life and love, when before it was so corrupt! I rejoice when I feel the strength to do the things that I was so weak to do prior to the change.

I thank the Lord! Every day! For there is progress when you change. There is progress when you say yes. There is progress when you decide to keep filling yourself up with the things of God rather than the things of this earth! You feel different. You act different. You talk different. You function different and you just live DIFFERENT! You are no longer the same old self.

That is the way God wants us to move ahead. He said in His Word, "BE YE RENEWED" in Ephesians 4:23. He wants us to be renewed, restored and rebuilt! That is my heart's way now. There is no other way for me. All else has passed and this is my new life.

In the opening of Proverbs, it tells us to KNOW, to PERCEIVE and to RECEIVE. This we shall do during our growth process.

> *To know wisdom and instruction, To perceive the words of understanding, To receive the instruction of wisdom, justice, judgment, and equity.* Proverbs 1:2-3 (New King James Version)

I know that God loves me, saved me and called me.

> *Therefore do not be unwise but understand what the will of the Lord is.* Ephesians 5:17 (New King James Version)

I perceive what God wants me to be, to say and to do.

Then Peter opened his mouth and said: "In truth, I perceive that God shows no partiality." Acts 10:34 (New King James Version)

I receive God's grace and strength in order to live this life.

For we are glad when we are weak and you are strong. And this we also pray, that you may be made complete. 2 Corinthians 13:9 (New King James Version)

My heart is not failing me now.
My soul is no longer tied to the past.
My mind recognizes the lies being told.
My strength is operating through the grace of God.

If you no longer want to walk defeated; no longer want to be tossed to and fro; no longer want to keep battling with the same old thing, then surrender it all to Him. Start seeking Him through prayer, fasting, worship, reading and working for the kingdom. If you want to see the change, then BE the change. It is time for us to start living the change IN GOD!

That is certainly possible. And it feels GREAT to be this free!

We keep working our way from renewal, restoration and into a rebuilt vessel!

REBUILD

To repair, especially to DISMANTLE and REASSEMBLE with new parts. To replace, restrengthen, reinforce, to revise, reshape or reorganize; to build again or freshen.

Build
Build up
Fix
Patch
Touch up
Overhaul
Reassemble
Recondition
Reconstruct
Refurbish
Administer
Give treatment
Medicate
Mend
Repair
Revamp
Supply

REBUILT: Beginning the Ending

PIECE 21
UNDER CONSTRUCTION

I believe that everyone has that moment in life where God is calling for a rebuild. It is when He takes us to a deeper and profound place in His presence. In order to do so, we go through a season where we are being dismantled in every way so that God can reassemble us with new parts. He takes the old and tears it down. It hurts. It is painful. Because those things that were built were mainly by choice. They are things we desired, loved, hoped for and even dreamed. In those things, many have nothing to do with the plans of God. In fact, it interferes with God's agenda. Therefore, He calls for a REBUILD. We are under construction!

When we come to the place where He is building, He takes us in a destination that is so fierce, and precise that we know without a shadow of a doubt this is it. All else is destroyed before it destroys us. We must pass through this destination.

There is no other way to get there without having to go through an off trail.

Driving down a long yet necessary trip by myself to Ohio left a lot of time to reflect. I passed through many areas that were "Under Construction" and had closed off roads. They also wait for the darkest hours to get the work on the road done. It is so frustrating because if you factor in your travel time you expect to pass through faster through the night watches. However, they do not shut down that path. People have to pass through. It is necessary. This is the only way to go. It can be a bit inconvenient, slow, noisy, scary and rough, but we proceed with much precaution.

There are always signs around us with warnings ahead even before we approach the working site. As we pass through the rough road, it may be at a reduced speed but the fixing needs to occur for the great big plan of an improved road. For us… there is a great big plan that He has of an improved and healthy life!

Eventually we get to the smooth road and it feels like you are driving in a space ship. Everything is going well and even fast. Times like this are constant for us, when we know which road we have to take. As we keep moving to where we need to go, there is always going to be the rough area to pass through to get to the smooth area. In addition, with all the signs in place, you will get to your destination. Even when the road moves from narrow to wide. So inconvenient… However, in the great scheme of things, it is all just necessary. Fixing needs to occur.

"But He knows the way that I take; when He has tried me, I shall come out as gold" Job 23:10 (New King James Version)

Isn't how this works with God too? During the most darkest times in our lives –He works the most construction!

We are like that in our walk of life. We still have to go through that direction. Especially when we make commitments! I made a commitment to be somewhere and this was the WAY to get there. There were moments of frustration, darkness and other times where it was smooth sailing. What an experience.

Through the journey, so many places were breathtaking. I was catching quick glimpses of amazing areas. I wish I could have stopped and had more time to appreciate all of

God's creation but I had to keep going. In this particular case, timing was essential for my arrival and departure.

I did get to see beautiful skies, the patches of rain, the sunset and the dark of the night.

I can determine at this point in my life, I have never been SO SURE of the road that I need to take. I have a great vehicle as my tool for travel. I have an amazing GPS! And I have an "Estimated Time of Arrival" so AT LEAST I have an idea more or less of when I am going to get there. If I keep moving down this road in this direction with the least amount of pit stops that should not delay my arrival. This is how I feel with God as my source. My mind is driven. My mind is steadfast on Him! The road I am taking is the road WITH GOD! I know what I am called to do. I know where I am assigned to be. I know WITH WHOM I am supposed to be there with and I am going to do my best.

I may make some mistakes along the way that cause delay because I am not a perfect person. But I do know this; I am going to do all things with God in my life and will always find that place in His presence where I completely belong with every good thing about me and with every flaw. I know that in the darkest times of my life is when most of the "road work" is being done to make me more refined and renewed. God is *rebuilding* me day by day and it is constant work. It is an ongoing construction site in my life. God is the master architect and has great blueprints of my life. I trust that He has outlined everything to perfection and know all His things will come to pass for me.

Under Construction

You will show me the path of life; In Your presence is fullness of joy, At Your right hand there are pleasures forevermore. Psalm 16:11 (New King James Version)

When I woke… I saw the dark road ahead. I remembered the different textures of the road as I drove through rough ground and smooth ground. In all of that, I have to do what I was supposed to do. It was worthwhile. As I do get to spend this time alone, I reflect on all the places in my life where God has taken me. I sometimes beat myself over the bad stuff but I quickly bring myself to that place where He has given us grace! Tremendous grace! And I do not want to take that for granted on my road trip. I want to acknowledge Him in all my ways. Even through things that were not the sharpest. I know He will love me no matter what and cover me with that grace. He took all my sins and burdens to the cross– PAST, PRESENT & FUTURE.

Through the construction, I am able to see His superstructure! He shows us the path, we take it and in it, we will have all the fullness that we need… He is the best builder there is! There is no other route to take but through His construction site. Just go through it.

"As they pass through the Valley of Baca, They make it a spring; The rain covers it with pools. They go from strength to strength; Each one appears before God in Zion." Psalm 84:6-7 (New King James Version)

You will no longer be detoured when you come into this place of surrender and building. God has dismantled it all, so that everything can be reassembled into the places they belong. Those promises come to pass.

I am not sure of all the horror stories, one can only imagine. Everyone has their own. But whatever you have been through in life God is the perfect architect. Let Him do the rebuilding. Even if they laugh at you, doubt you or talk about you… the work that He is doing in you will be evident. It will shut the mouths and send the enemy fleeing seven ways when they try to come up against you.

Your ministry is not ruined. Your destiny is not over. Your career is not through. You did not lose your mind. During the renewal and recovery, He placed you firm. Now you are in a spacious place. He brought you out so you can testify. Now this is between you and God. You are a new vessel for the kingdom. What God is going to do in your life will be amazing and continually life changing. Others will want what you have. Others will want to go where you go. Others will want to hear what you hear. Others will want to see what you see. You are going to be like a tree—a huge source for others. You will point them in the direction of God.

No matter how many times we try at this thing, we have one thing in common with Christ. We can start again!

Whether it is a great start or tough beginning?

Smooth sailing or rocky roads?

Easy journey or crazy obstacles?

As you continue to pass through it all, you will go unseared. As you walk with the Lord your God, no evil shall befall you. No plague shall come near you. No serpent shall poison you [Psalm 91]. Through any fire, you will not be burned. Just like the three Hebrew young men in the book of Daniel, so shall you be if you stay trusting God.

Stand on His word. Stand on the precious promises. For daily as you continue to be fierce in your walk, there will be those moments that such will come against you. But be of good courage and be of good cheer, because you shall overcome any obstacle that you face. God is on your side.

To sear is to burn or char the surface of; to mark with a branding iron; to burn or scorch injuriously or painfully; to make callous or unfeeling; harden; to dry up or wither; parch; or a mark or scar made by searing.

Through His word, He is reminding you that you will not be seared or scorched. You will not run dry or wither up. There will be no mark or scar held over you to remind you of your past traumas.

In using the same scripture of Isaiah – **New International Version**, this reminds us we go unharmed.

> *When you pass through the waters, I will be with you; and when you pass through the rivers, they will not sweep over you. When you walk through the fire, you will not be burned; the flames will not set you ablaze.*
> Isaiah 43:2

The bible does not say that we will never pass through it or that this year will be trial free. But it does promise that we will go unseared. We will go untouched. We will go through any situation and come out victorious.

When you pass through the waters—He is with you.

When it gets higher and you pass through the rivers—He is with you. It is not going to drown you.

The past will not drown you. The hurt will not drown you. The arguments will not drown you. The gossip will not drown you. The lies will not drown you. The bills will not drown you. The enemy CANNOT drown you— stick to the promises! That will elevate you. When you know what God told you! Rest in that great calm.

When you walk through that fire—you will NOT be burned. You are not even going to look like you went through it. You are going to be rejoicing, peaceful, laughing and standing stronger than ever before. This year will be the one that you stand the highest. People will look at you and wonder why you are so filled with the Spirit of joy and they will want what you have.

Many times God will CAUSE you to walk through it just so that all can SEE that you are unharmed by it! That you are even blessed by it! That even for many of what looks like a setback is a set up for God to lift you higher.

As a child of God, He is taking you through. As the problems of life press through ALL, the promises of God are fulfilled through ALL—if you stick to that! Know what God promised you. A victorious life my friend! That is promised for us.

Be thankful and spread the good news of what He is doing in you. Motivate others in this time, even if you feel like you need motivation. Pray for others when you need intercession. Encourage those around you when you feel like you need it too. For as you do all those things you will come to see that God carried you through it all, so that you can share it. This is our testimony. This is our constructed life. You have been unseared.

> ***He divided the sea and caused them to pass through, And He made the waters stand up like a heap.*** Psalm 78:13 (New King James Version)

> ***Then the high officers, officials, governors, and advisers crowded around them and saw that the fire had not touched them. Not a hair on their heads was singed, and their clothing was not scorched. They didn't even smell of smoke!*** Daniel 3:27 (New Living Translation)

REBUILT: Beginning the Ending

PIECE 22
ALL GROWN UP

Maybe I didn't have the wedding of the century.
Maybe you weren't there to walk me down the aisle.
Maybe you weren't there to see my first child born…or then the next.
Maybe you weren't there for graduation.
Maybe you weren't there for prom.
Maybe you weren't there for my first fall or my first job.
Maybe you weren't there for it all.

Maybe none of that ever matters, just as long as I am here for you now.

I am all grown up, I was Daddy's little girl. I battled with the thought to come here. For a major life turning procedure. It is so hard to turn the tables of a schedule. Yet waking up I could feel something so unsettling in me and I wasn't sure what that was. So here, I am now, moved heaven and earth's schedule to be a part of this moment. Because it mattered. It mattered that much. I know I did the right thing.

I could hear your loud voice. Asking someone where Registration was. When you walked in the room, your eyes scanned the unfamiliar, the familiar and then your eyes saw me. I know you are strong, yet scared. I know you are tough yet weak. I know that you are here and I am there. But the moment your eyes saw me…you noted, "Daddy's little girl." The tears stung your already bloodshot red eyes. You moved away from the registration desk and walked fast to greet me. "How'd you do it? I can't believe you are here!" A smile worth millions is something you could never replace. You were quickly comforted in a moment of uneasy despair. You cried. That moment became monumental.

So despite all the maybes, nothing else is as important as our present – for that is what we can influence. That is what we can CREATE! That is what we can change! For all the rest is canceled out in the moment of our present… I am still daddy's little girl. I am important. I do matter in your life. Being here makes the difference. Even though I have my mom, I also have my dad. It took the two of you to make me. I love you both individually. The past matters NOT. I am here today supporting you both because you are the only parents God gave me.

Don't be mad. Don't be jealous. Love goes a long way. It is the strongest force that moves the world – the force that is our God. God is love. And He has given it to us to extend to others. I am thankful. You did a great job. You did your best. You showed me how to keep the faith and keep it through it all. Every time I am near you – that's what counts the most. You give me all the love I need that makes up for the past. I am here. I am not going away. I am not full of regrets.

> **This is the Message I've been set apart to proclaim as preacher, emissary, and teacher. It's also the cause of all this trouble I'm in. But I have no regrets. I couldn't be more sure of my ground—the One I've trusted in can take care of what He's trusted me to do right to the end.** 2 Timothy 1:11-12 (The Message)

I am with my dad now…sitting by the bedside as he just had two major surgeries back to back. He is in recovery. This is my sole purpose in life. He has entrusted us to do things right until the end. This is the right thing. To support each other and be there positively in each other's lives. To make things better and put an effort to do what is good and wholesome. This is wholesome for me now. I miss my family at home, but I am really appreciating the time here with my dad for this recovery and time with my other immediate family. We are catching up. Lots of hugs, laughter, and sharing.

My dad is a trooper. Despite all the pain and discomfort, he is really trying to pull through bravely. He sleeps, he snores, he wakes and yells about the pain. But the worst part is over. The first part to do something necessary has taken place and it was NOT easy. It had to be done. We all need to go through times that are trying so that we can have a healthy and better life.

Daddy –I know you appreciate me here.

Father…my Lord –I know you appreciate me here too.

I am Daddy's little girl…here to support and do what is right until the end with the best of my ability that You have given me.

I hope I made you proud.

I love you!

In the process of rebuilding, many times you will have to visit those past pains and hurts. Paula White stated in her teaching of "Breaking Ungodly Soul Ties" the following:

> "Why do we keep coming up empty? Recreating sick cycles and patterns when Christ died for all of that. Until you take the ax to the root, you will never have a real deliverance. You will keep putting Band-Aids on broken elbows. This is the time of establishing a true wholeness. Psychology and counseling are good but cannot take you beyond time and space. Only the spirit of God can lead you out of time and space to an internal realm. Sometimes things were so deeply embedded that you don't even know where it happened. But only

the Spirit of God can take you in a moment of time where that injury occurred and bring a balm of Gilead so that there is closure to that place that was wounded."

Stop putting Band-Aids. Stop wrapping up your issues. Maybe it is time for you to put closure on the wound too. What was the thing that caused you the most pain? The piece that needs the true healing and the true forgiveness to take place.

I found it through visiting those places where I was severely wounded... can you find it too?

It is not easy to visit those places, because they are filled with the deepest pain. But the deeper that pain is the deeper the space that God will fill and bring that everlasting healing.

I realize that my mom had to work overtime to do many things on her own because my dad was no longer in the home. My mom had to fight her own wounds and battles. My mom had to hold the baton for the home and that was hard. I will always be thankful for her. I have my mom with me now. I take care of her now. I provide what she needs when she wants. I am in a position now to bless her because she deserves to be blessed. I can see that even as a member of our home, she is still holding a baton. She helps me during the week. She cooks, cleans and helps always around the house. Even as she is hobbling with a bad knee.

My husband adores her, they talk all the time. She gives him foot massages and prepares his things too. As the kids were growing she always helped to watch them--no questions asked, she just did it. Our kids are her kids and that is a priority for her. Enough said. They love her so much. Sometimes I think even more than me--and I am okay with that because she deserves that love from a hard-pressed life.

Her upbringing was hard and I don't hold any grudges upon her for the past. I decided not to be a prisoner of my past. In a prison, there is nothing to do really, except be confined to one particular area. I have chosen to be free, live and progress!

I understand that the way that I am, I did inherit from both my parents. I would never imagine to even see what God is doing in both of them separately.

If you knew my mom back in the day—you would be like, "WATCH OUT!" Today, she is different.

I see the change.

My dad was on a path to wellness after fighting liver and kidney cancer. My mom is on a path to wellness and wholeness after surrendering her life to God. She is a member of our church. She reads the bible every day. She prays to God and is seeking to grow even at her age now. She is being fruitful. She is learning to engage with new church family and friends. I am proud of her. She is a woman worthy of honor and will always be my Proverbs 31 type of gal! I love her to pieces!!!

MOMMY you did it! You are the BEST mom anyone

could ask for. I wouldn't trade you for the world. You have two blessed kids--one serving our country as a US Coast Guard and one serving the Lord as a US Ambassador and pastor of a church. Wow! Look at what you have sown in us! You are beyond amazing mom! I love you.

For all those reflecting on the mommy that God gave them, just know that God always knows what He is doing. We appreciate the good with the bad. We live and we learn. We grow and we sow. We remember beyond the darkest days that they are still a person just like us, that God sent His Son to die on the cross for.

God gave me two parents and that was nothing I could change but appreciate today. As a rebuilt vessel, I am all grown up. I am Daddy's Little Girl – my Heavenly Father. You knew what you were doing when you made me.

> *You made all the delicate, inner parts of my body and knit me together in my mother's womb. Thank you for making me so wonderfully complex! Your workmanship is marvelous—how well I know it. You watched me as I was being formed in utter seclusion, as I was woven together in the dark of the womb. You saw me before I was born. Every day of my life was recorded in your book. Every moment was laid out before a single day had passed. How precious are your thoughts about me, O God. They cannot be numbered!* Psalm 139:13-17 [New International Version]

REBUILT: Beginning the Ending

PIECE 23

THE BROKEN ONE

We can always find those moments to enjoy the remains of summer. Blue skies, breezy weather, shining sun with its rays lighting up the sand and keeping warm our skin. Everything looks lovely. The tides from last week brought in a whole array of shells!!! Different sizes, shapes and bold colors. They are each unique. There are even some broken ones washed up from the shore. If you go far enough, you'll pull up some of the most amazing shells! We can make a collection of them for display.

She scoops down to get a different shell after shell that catches the eyes. Water is about ankle deep and not strong at all. Just enough to push the shells a bit so they glisten under the shallow water. This one stands out... It is white and blue... Perfectly striped all the way to the end but it's broken!!! She tosses it back in the water. Oddly enough, she feels an inner conviction and thought, "God wouldn't throw me away if I was broken!" So she stoops back down digging into the water and sand for that broken one! Oh how lovely! She showed it to me and told me the story. I said, "But with all the shells you have here this broken one is the most beautiful one of them all! Look!" I tilt it a bit so you see the broken side and it's that cobalt blue that some other steady beach goers had mentioned. The part where it was broken had a beautiful blue color and not like the others.

She agreed and gave it to me saying, "Here, take it!" I said, "That one is yours, I can't take that!" We were like two little girls debating over the best seashells!!! And laughing out loud! She said, "Stop just take it, I got that one for you!"

It is already in my vase at home with many others. The first person I showed all my seashells to said, that broken one is very pretty!

You see! That is how we are! We may think we are useless, no good, of no value, cast off, forgotten, neglected, emptied, deserted, alone, shameful, indifferent and the like... Yet God sees us as beautiful! When we think there is nothing else left, we could do with ourselves… God sees there is more! So much more!

> *This is the word that came to Jeremiah from the Lord: "Go down to the potter's house, and there I will give you my message." So I went down to the potter's house, and I saw him working at the wheel. But the pot he was shaping from the clay was marred in his hands; so the potter formed it into another pot, shaping it as seemed best to him. Then the word of the Lord came to me. 6 He said, "Can I not do with you, Israel, as this potter does?" declares the Lord. "Like clay in the hand of the potter, so are you in my hand, Israel.* Jeremiah 18:1-6 (New International Version)

He will never throw us away. He will never think there is nothing left of us. He will never forget about us. He will never think that we are useless because of something that happened to us that caused us to be broken. In fact, it is quite the opposite, where He takes the broken ones and He makes them the most beautiful ones. The ones that have the best testimonies, the best smiles, the best stories, and the best victories come out of their brokenness.

You may feel broken, you may look broken, you may act broken but when it comes to God, the broken one is the most beautiful one… He will never cast you off.

> *"Do not fear, for you will not be ashamed; Neither be disgraced, for you will not be put to shame; For you will forget the shame of your youth, And will not remember*

the reproach of your widowhood anymore." Isaiah 54:4 (New King James Version)

You know even the worst people in the Bible were protected by God and He used them in powerful ways. If you look at Cain after he had killed his brother Abel, God protected him because he still saw him as a valuable life despite what he did wrong [Genesis 4].

Apostle Paul consented in the deaths of many but God consented in the life of Paul and used him in a powerful way to uphold many churches and bring the gospel to the gentiles [Acts 9]. Even King David made a mess of things and God kept him all throughout his days. He even wrote, "I am feeble and severely broken; I groan because of the turmoil of my heart [Psalms 38:8]."

So no matter how broken you may feel or look, to God you are His choice! And it is time for Him to put you on display… He is collecting all the broken pieces of your life. All the shattered moments. All the things that hurt you the most in your process, so that He can shine His glory through your broken story. As we reflect of the lives of others through the Word of God, there will be moments where you will see His work in your life, even through the absolute worst events.

It is okay to be the broken one, we all have been there. And we shall see the beauty of it all in God's timetable.

The Broken One

This is a serious section because no one really talks about the stuff that's hard to talk about.

Like all these things that we envision as great do not become great in the blink of an eye. What happens in a course of 20+ years is not all sun and rays!

Especially at home, work, marriage and child rearing. Can I just openly share, for this is my story...

What about the times that a family vacation was ruined?

How about the times you argued all the way there and back on a 24-hour road trip?

How about the silent treatment for hours or days that you don't speak to your loved ones?

How about when home feels like prison and not a palace or when you feel like a child and not a spouse.

What if you feel abused, used and unloved in a place that is supposed to be loving and sacred?

What about the times you were discredited, devalued or dishonored in your own home or relationship? Who wants to talk about that?

What about the sleepless nights?

Or the times you cried yourself to sleep all alone or even by a spouse in bed? Single people feel weight and so do the married at times of war.

What about the times where everything goes unnoticed?

What about the forgotten anniversaries, birthdays and appreciation or recognition of huge accomplishments? Doesn't all that make your heart just sink?

When you're so excited about something and share it with your loved one and get, "ehhh" as they have their face buried in their cell phone?

How about when your new blouse or shoes go unnoticed; when your haircut isn't noticed or you shed a couple of pounds and told you look fat!

What about you liking the heat and they like the cold?

If you like Chinese and they like Italian? You watch romance and they prefer comedy.

You eat popcorn and loud candy and they survive on water.

What about all the rude comments that tear you down mentally, physically, emotionally and spiritually?

How about waking up every morning to wipe someone

else's piss off the toilet seat before you have to go and you have to put the cap on the toothpaste as a daily routine. Those little things that happen day after day actually become extremely frustrating.

And so what about the intense moments when your lifelong partner feels like your lifelong enemy?

Isn't that all a violation of some sort?

Ok maybe it is just me. What about all that?

Let it be the woman or the man, it will happen to any HUMAN so God sent us the Son of Man to conquer it all.

All these questions we have, God answer us.

People think we share too much, but this is our story. It has not been an easy one. We did not become super saving Christians overnight. That took some time. We had to go from stage to stage, moment to moment and fight to fight!

I remember some years back, we had to ride to work together my husband and I because we worked in the same place, we only needed one car at the time. But I tell you, those days riding every day weren't always glorious ones. I do recall one time on a colder day that I had rushed to get in the passenger seat with my bowl of cereal. He drove to work while talking on the phone and kept chit chatting along the way enjoying the conversation that he was having. By the time we got to the workplace, he stopped to let me out on the side of the street. When I opened the door to get out my foot was caught on the strap of my messenger bag causing me to fly forward out of the car. The cereal bowl flew in the air and shattered in several pieces. I heard the sound of the utensil also hit the ground as my face hit flat as well. My palms were quickly scrapped and I was quickly shocked by the sudden fall. I looked back and my husband never ended the phone conversation or came out to help and see if I was okay. He just reached his head to peek at me with a weird expression and he said, "What's wrong with you—are you alright?" A stranger came quickly and picked me up. I looked at my husband and said, "THANKS, I am okay. Have a great day." I slammed the door shut.

We both slammed the door shut on each other several times in our relationship.

I remember moments like that were I fell flat on my face, when I needed help or that I needed to be pampered in some way. But I also remember the moment that we sat across the table in a diner and I had to tell him that I was unfaithful to him. I remember the tears stinging his eyes, his heart and his soul. I remember that pain as well. He took his fist to wipe his tears. We were both upset, hurt and angry with each other for many things. I had gotten the worst from him and he had gotten the worst of the worst from me. For not only did that pain sting him, but it also stung our family in such a way.

This is a difficult story that we had repeatedly walked down. But I can tell you this—God renewed us, restored us and rebuilt this family back from the ground up. We have helped countless couples and people as we talk through the healing of our relationship. We have had private counseling, professional counseling and Christian counseling for years. We talk about many things that people will never dare to discuss. But I do know we are not the only ones that have been here. I found many books on dealing with marriage, where I could read other stories that brought healing. We look to the scriptures repeatedly and pray them over our home. I know I have often felt like the black sheep of the family—but I would have never come to know the depth of the scriptures as it speaks in the book of Isaiah. That is my redemption book. I thank God that despite all of our hardships, He spoke over us repeatedly!

So not only did we never give up when we felt like giving up, but GOD NEVER GAVE UP ON OUR UNION. There was a place where we found healing and restoration. There was a place that we found renewal for us. There was a place where we could be completely dismantled so that we could be assembled the RIGHT WAY.

Truth became our shield and buckler. We are a broken home. But a broken home that has been rebuilt. I would say that our relationship is unique. So many ill things but we have learned to laugh again, talk again, trust again, spend time together richly, love each other again intimately bit by bit. We really trusted God and continue to place that trust on Him.

The broken one has now become the blessed one, the redeemed one, and the one that will be a place of safety for many. IT would be an injustice to exclude the countless passages in the book of Isaiah where we found God speaking to us. So I must conclude this chapter with that.

Please take the time to study these passages...especially in the New King James Version, New International Version and The Message translation. All three brought more depth and clarity.

God is a Restorer to the Broken—A Builder to those fallen. Thank you God for placing your healing hand over us, and I know you have done that for many! For when I thought we were utterly destroyed and beyond fixing, You reminded us that You did this just for us!

> *Who believes what we've heard and seen? Who would have thought God's saving power would look like this? The servant grew up before God—a scrawny seedling, a scrubby plant in a parched field. There was nothing attractive about him, nothing to cause us to take a second look. He was looked down on and passed over, a man who suffered, who knew pain firsthand. One look at him and people turned away. We looked down on him, thought he was scum. But the fact is, it was our pains he carried— our disfigurements, all the things wrong with us. We thought he brought it on himself, that God was punishing him for his own failures. But it was our sins that did that to him, that ripped and tore and crushed him—our sins! He took the punishment, and that made us whole. Through his bruises we get healed. We're all like sheep who've wandered off and gotten lost. We've all done our own thing, gone our own way. And God has piled all our sins, everything we've done wrong, on him, on him. He was beaten, he was tortured, but he didn't say a word. Like a lamb taken to*

The Broken One

be slaughtered and like a sheep being sheared, he took it all in silence. Justice miscarried, and he was led off—and did anyone really know what was happening? He died without a thought for his own welfare, beaten bloody for the sins of my people. They buried him with the wicked, threw him in a grave with a rich man, Even though he'd never hurt a soul or said one word that wasn't true. Still, it's what God had in mind all along, to crush him with pain. The plan was that he give himself as an offering for sin so that he'd see life come from it—life, life, and more life. And God's plan will deeply prosper through him. Out of that terrible travail of soul, he'll see that it's worth it and be glad he did it. Through what he experienced, my righteous one, my servant, will make many "righteous ones," as he himself carries the burden of their sins. Therefore I'll reward him extravagantly—the best of everything, the highest honors—Because he looked death in the face and didn't flinch, because he embraced the company of the lowest. He took on his own shoulders the sin of the many, he took up the cause of all the black sheep. Isaiah 53 [The Message Translation]

REBUILT: Beginning the Ending

PIECE 24

IN GOD'S COLLAGE

A huge part of my summer was spent spending time with me. I know that seems pretty selfish but I did have the opportunity to do so. My husband took on a summer job and both my kids were working as well. I also accepted a flex-schedule at my job so I had longer days but leading to three day weekends. It barely rained at all this past summer so I was able to spend the time right by the beach. How beautiful it was. I was able to see an ocean of possibilities before me. I was able to renew myself by spending time away from everything else. I was able to revive and refresh. I brought good books, worship music and rested on pure white sand. I took long walks by the ocean. I fell in love with Long Island.

There was nothing but a beautiful ocean, white sand, gentle breeze, sound of the shore, open space, different shells and stones. I scoop down and begin collecting them because I know when I put them together they are going to look beautiful ... For they are all different in their own way, maybe some similar, some cracked, some not, some transparent, some with colors, some dark, some large, some tiny, some ragged but all together they make a beautiful collection of art.

Just like us. I think we are very much the same way actually. This Scripture tells us in 2 Corinthians 3:18, "But we all, with unveiled face, beholding as in a mirror of the glory of the Lord, are being transformed into the *same image* from glory to glory, just as by the Spirit of the Lord."

Now the word of God tells us that we are all going to be transformed into the same image and not only that but that it is going to be glorious. Right now, we all contain our own level of glory that God has given to us because He is IN US. He tells us that when we are all transformed we actually become one and that makes us go from glory to glory.

New levels.
Many levels.
Unending levels.

For how exciting that can be for us when we have that perspective. Sometimes we look at who we are, where we are and then begin to have doubt. We get discouraged, always thinking that we have nothing to give because of what we have been through or are still going through. But with this, God actually takes those things and gives us a beautiful story. He gives us the ability and makes us able to stand strong [Ephesians 6]. Then we come to realize that nothing was able to take us down because we had something glorious inside of us all along.... G O D!

That glory is what God placed inside of us to be able to endure any trial and any circumstance. With others, then we are also able to come together and become EVEN STRONGER! As I was at the beach, I kept collecting the rocks and shells and putting them in this plastic bag. With every piece, the bag continued to get heavier and heavier. It had so much weight to it from the many shells and stones. So I thought, the same way we continue to pile up together –we actually become stronger!

We just need to get rid of any mindset that tells us that we are all alone, that we have nobody else, or that we are better off being by ourselves... when this is never the case with God! He created togetherness. That's why He is even part of a Holy Trinity!

FATHER
SON
HOLY SPIRIT

In the same way, He wants us to function with togetherness and with power. This comes with unity...like the people had in the Book of Acts! With that being said, we also have to keep in mind that everybody is **different.** Maybe some people are even more similar than others and others could be very much opposite. In any case, we will have something beautiful on our own and when we come together, it is MORE beautiful and MORE glorified. The Bible tells us in 1 Corinthians 1:31 that, "He who glories, let him glory in the Lord." That is what we glory about. We glory about what God does inside of us, we glory about what He does in us, what He does through us and for us. It is what He wants to do with the body of Christ through broken and flawed vessels like us. When we all come together and share our stories. In this way, we actually make an exquisite collage.

When you think of a collage, it is defined as a technique of composing a work of art by pasting on a single surface various materials not normally associated with one another, as newspaper clippings, parts of photographs, theater tickets, and fragments of an envelope. When we come together as one, as a body of Christ, we actually become God's collage! This is where He takes **all of the different pieces** and places us **together** in a single surface called the church. This is known as the body of Christ! This is God's church. This is God's ultimate purposed. This is what God is calling fellowship and having an open communion. This is God's collage and God's artwork. For how beautiful it is when we can all come together as one, take all our broken pieces, all our differences and put them together.

Every year we celebrate friendship day! On this day we take a moment to acknowledge, recognize and appreciate the people that God has placed beside us, even if there are some that are more difficult than others. The truth is when you find difficulty –you actually discover **more** beauty. Because as hard as it was to put it together, we were able to do it despite any obstacles, barriers or differences. It is possible. That is like-mindedness. It is called acceptance. With my closest friends, we have conquered very difficult circumstances. Now we are called "best" friends.

Just like all the shells and rocks that I collected for the purpose of decorating, as I put them inside the bowl filled with sand [which is the single surface] I took a picture because together it actually looked very beautiful. All the beautiful and different pieces placed in the same surface became a unique collection of art for a nice display in my dining room. I shared the photos, and they agreed. Wow, how BEAUTIFUL! I took the broken and torn pieces that actually hurt your feet stepping on them and placed them in a single place for an eye-catching display.

This must be a good thing when it is a God-thing. Take your life and place it before God. Come to a place in your life where you can mesh with others…He wants to make a collage. Why would you think for one moment that your piece and contribution wouldn't make a difference–when it really does?

You are God's design.

You are a part of God's collage.

You are a work of art.

You have something unique to contribute.

You have a story that is life impacting and worth sharing.

Every day is a new day – fresh mercies and not just on this friendship day. But a day to make a difference. Share what God has given you, share your time, your words, your smile, your hugs… There is so much that you can give. Since God is the Creator of all things, then He knows what He is doing with this arrangement… What a collage, when it was designed by God.

Days and weeks went by and I felt myself smiling again, laughing again, sharing again and coming back to a happier home. There was that ocean of possibilities before me. I had a choice to do something good and something better. I had an opportunity to make things improved for us. All I could see was this river.

There is a river whose streams make glad the city of God, the holy place where the Most High dwells. Psalm 46:4 (New International Version)

As I looked upon a beautiful ocean that seemed endless, I got to rest in such a serene and tranquil place for days at a time. I escape from the busy city, work, home, church, and everything else that keeps me tied up. It is my getaway from all. It is a time for me to recover from life itself.

Mike Shea wrote a phrase in a recovery journal: "When my faith is tested, can it be trusted?" It makes you ponder on the possibilities that are presented before us. In order to walk through those doors of opportunities we need

FAITH for real. An unmovable faith, trust, confidence and stillness to wait for the right ones to walk through.

I sat through a teaching given by my husband at our church and I got a little emotional at the words. I reflect upon my own personal story and think… Why does everything have to be so narrow sometimes? It must be part of God's collage.

> *"Enter by the narrow gate; for wide is the gate and broad is the way that leads to destruction, and there are many who go in by it. Because narrow is the gate and difficult is the way which leads to life, and there are few who find it."* Matthew 7:13-14 (New King James Version)

So narrow it is, and beyond our control. Perhaps this is just the place where many doors close so that we walk through the best one given by God. That way it won't be so confusing. We often come to those spots in life and become so unsure of what to do… When it looks like many doors are closing and we are losing opportunity.

Surely, we need faith.

We can come to that understanding that God is limitless. That there is nothing impossible for Him because His Word declares such in Matthew 19:46 and Luke 1:37. Yet when the problems start to arise, we begin to lose sight of all that God purposed for us. We know His will for us demands for blessing, increase and favor. But what do we do when we experience the opposite? This is where we really need to put that faith to practice. When all of our faith will be tested.

> ***"For a great and effective door has opened to me, and there are many adversaries."*** I Corinthians 16:9 (New King James Version)

See there is a door that opens for us.

A door of blessing.

A door of increase.

A door of favor.

This was the door for our healing and restoration. A door that contains our inheritance and promise!!! We just need to do what God tells us to do… Even if we have to wait on Him, despite the obstacles that WILL surely arise! For when the doors open that are going to be effective, just as the Word declares, we are definitely going to have some heavy opposition. Why else would we have such a fight? This way our victory is going to be such a reason to celebrate.

I am sure the Israelites felt opposition before the parting of the red sea.

I am sure Abraham felt opposition when God asked him to sacrifice his only son that was supposed to be the heir!

I am sure Joseph felt opposition when he was thrown into a pit by his brothers!

I am sure the army with David felt opposition when they

burned down their place of rest in Ziklag and carried off their women and children as hostage!

I am sure the three Hebrew men felt opposition when they were thrown into a fiery furnace that was turned up seven times stronger!

Lastly, I am sure Jesus Himself felt opposition when He was betrayed by one of His own disciples. I am sure He felt more opposition being scourged. And I am sure He felt the worst kind of opposition hanging on the cross.

Everyone encounters and feels the weight of opposition but it is in knowing what you are promised that really takes you through. Our short-term pain must be felt in order for us to receive our long-term gain [Mike Shea]. We just need to use our faith. The possibilities are endless when we put our trust in God. We just need to walk through that one narrow door that will lead to all the rest!

Just trust God.

Use your faith.

Believe that promise and place in God is yours despite everything that is happening in the interim. Our focus should always be the promise and not the problem. Our focus should be the opportunity and not the opposition. Our focus should be our faith and not fear that tries to paralyze us. The promises of God are sure to happen –that is a guarantee. It just hurts when we also have the guarantee of opposition! The good news is… We will get through it and to it! That door may look narrow, feel narrow and sound narrow but it is the exact place to take you to the ocean of God's possibilities! You will be blessed beyond what you could think of. For His ways are so much higher than ours [Isaiah 55:9].

> ***Now to Him who is able to [carry out His purpose and] do superabundantly more than all that we dare ask or think [infinitely beyond our greatest prayers, hopes, or dreams], according to His power that is at work within us.*** (Amplified)

> ***He will do immeasurably, exceedingly and abundantly according to the power that works in us*** [Ephesians 3:20].

Just walk through those tight places, for it will bring you to the harvest of ABUNDANCE!

An ocean of possibilities is our promise!

PIECE 25
REMINDERS ALONG THE WAY

This image was taken from my super camera on one of the weekends that I spend in Long Island. I was amazed at how God brought such this fascinating flying bug in front of me to see. I am not sure how many actual reminders that we really need but I guess enough until we get that it is an all-powerful God that is sending them all.

> *You have been Christians a long time, now and you ought to be teaching others, but instead you have dropped back to the place where you need someone to*

teach you all over again the very principles in God's Word. You are like babies who can drink only milk, not old enough for solid food. Hebrews 5:12 (The Living Bible)

We have these moments where we drop back to the place where we need someone to show us all over again. How many times do we drop back? How many reminders do we need? How many prayer meetings or bible studies? How many signals and confirmations are we seeking? Anything more than twice, pretty much seals the deal [Genesis 41:32]. Yet God will constantly send as many reminders along the way–not in some bad way–but just enough to let us know that He is with us for every step that we make towards our wholeness.

God used this fascinating flying bug at the women's conference that changed my life. I will never forget this one because each message shared was based on discovering our true identity in Christ. The word that was delivered from each of the speakers was very profound. Each session spoke to our unique existence and purpose in life. The message that affected me the most was the last one–about the butterfly. She shared about how we go from all these stages in our walk with God. She explained the entire process of the butterfly and how we are like that as Christians. We go from various stages until we get to a unique and beautifully designed butterfly.

- ☐ There is the beginning stage as an egg.
- ☐ The slow stage of the caterpillar.

- ☐ The pupa stage also known as the cocooning.
- ☐ The stage of breaking out into the butterfly.

This is all a process of TRANS-FORMATION [the act or process of transforming; the state of being transformed; change in form, appearance, nature, or character].

I think I cried so much hearing about the caterpillar stage. I felt like a lot of my progress and growth had been so slow. I felt like a baby again. Just like the scripture spoke of in Hebrews 5–we ought to be teachers and now we need to be spoon fed all over again. How humiliating! How frustrating! How upsetting my whole soul felt to be in a place where I needed to be reminded AGAIN! Yet – this was actually the most liberating experience for me in my whole life. I was okay with being the baby. I was okay with this new birth type of experience. I was so free inside to know that I always have a fresh start with God every day. I felt the presence of God in such an amazing way. I left that place with a new heart, a new vision, a new focus and a new fire that was shut up in my bones [Jeremiah 20:9].

The strangest thing happened though. My flight was delayed due to a snowstorm back home and I had to stay another day. I wound up in a childcare ER. As I waited in the lobby for my sister-in-law to have her son cared for, I dozed off. When I woke, there was a cartoon playing on the lobby screen. It was actually showing a yellow caterpillar being transformed. The cocooning and then into this butterfly in golden yellow. I knew God was reminding me of the message. I kept this in my heart as a personal sign for me. Then when I got back home finally, I had to work the same day. Within a few hours, I get a random text from a friend that had no idea about the conference. She sent me a picture of a yellow caterpillar! I said to myself..."Wow God! Seriously! I get it...no more signs."

Since the women's conference, I have another reminder for me. In Long Island, we get to this museum for Sunday brunch before I leave to go back home and I take the picture. It was a yellow butterfly that landed right in front of me over some flowers. I have seen butterflies of course but not like this. This butterfly was huge...beautiful...and YELLOW! It buzzed and flicked its wings repeatedly over the flowers and did not leave its location. I was able to take several shots of the butterfly with my camera. It was beautiful. But most importantly, I thought how much more God was beautiful to me, that this was sent my way as another little reminder that He was with me. It could have been any other color...but it was another exact reminder for me. Yellow–for this signifies hope, peace, intellect, and wisdom. All of this to make huge milestone decisions in my life—a yellow butterfly as a symbol. I can affirm, all throughout my own unique transformation process in life, He is with me.

In this same way, we all have our own individual process of life – our stages of learning, growth and transformation. Throughout this all, we have our identity. We have acquired things over life that have taught us, shaped us and made us who we are. No matter which way our process goes, God is in the midst of it all. We should never feel ashamed of the baby steps either. As slow as we walk sometimes, we still move forward. There is a time where we may need to be fed that milk again. Milk is great. It is healthy for our nourishment and growth. This gives us a balance in our life. We will ALWAYS have those highs and lows. It is just a thing called LIFE! We have to learn to embrace all that…the good times and the bad. We always have to go through the dark days…that way we can appreciate when we do get to the light.

Let us receive the constant reminders. These reminders let us know that God is following us every step along the way. We are never doing all this on our own strength or effort. God propels us into our destiny and purpose….He even uses those bad days to glorify all the good things that He does on our behalf.

Be reminded! Be renewed! Be restored! Be rebuilt!

We need it all the time. All along the way…through each stage of our life. Never stop reminding us Lord. Keep showing us through signs and wonders. Show us through prayer. Show us through Your Word.

> ***Nevertheless, brethren, I have written more boldly to you on some points, as reminding you, because of the grace given to me by God,*** Romans 15:15 (New King James Version)

> ***For this reason I have sent Timothy to you, who is my beloved and faithful son in the Lord, who will remind you of my ways in Christ, as I teach everywhere in every church.*** 1 Corinthians 4:17 (New King James Version)

> *Therefore, I remind you to stir up the gift of God, which is in you through the laying on of my hands.* Timothy 1:6 (New King James Version)

> *For this reason, I will not be negligent to remind you always of these things, though you know and are established in the present truth. Yes, I think it is right, as long as I am in this tent, to stir you up by reminding you,* 2 Peter 1:12, 13 (New King James Version)

I am so glad for all the reminders… for it continues to bring life to the hidden gift that was always in me.

PIECE 26

LET IT BE

In order for me to survive and allow God to do a continual building I have to do these five things:

- ☐ Trust
- ☐ Dwell
- ☐ Feed
- ☐ Delight
- ☐ Commit

These are five major elements for structure during the process. They are found in Psalm 37:3-5, "Trust in the Lord, and do good; Dwell in the land and feed on His faithfulness. Delight yourself also in the Lord and He shall give you the desires of your heart. Commit your way to the lord, Trust also in Him, and He shall bring it to pass." Then comes a prayer to God, "We're going to vet this out together, I don't care how long it takes at this point. For I don't even know how long that will be. I have been asking, questioning and wondering, but this is it. I have reached the end of my rope. I have reached the point of no return. This is reality and so be it. Let it be. This is now letting go." I think this is how I clearly see that there is nothing else left to do but **TRUST** [*reliance on the integrity, strength, ability, surety of a person or thing*]. I am going to let it all out and all go until it has all gone out. For this is my new hope. God is not going anywhere, He will not leave me or forsake me. I will **dwell** [*to live or stay as permanent residence; reside; continue, linger over; emphasize*] in the presence of God for I know He is with me. God is my real coping mechanism, my shoulder to cry on, my arm for when I need strength and the one who holds me up when I feel none. I will **feed** [*supply with nourishment; satisfy; provide as food, necessary materials for development*] on His faithfulness. I will feed on His word day and night. Every tear shed is one He knows all too well and very much familiar with all grief. I am not afraid. When all of it comes, I will release it all and hold on to none of it until it has all gone out of me. I will **delight** [*high degree of pleasure and enjoyment*] myself in the Lord and in His word. He is my source of strength. He is my hope. He is my joy now. All things are new. I will fix my eyes on Jesus as the Word declares in Hebrews 3:1. My relationship with God is getting stronger by the day. He is building me up again and I will **commit** [*to give trust in or charge; pledge*] to that work in me.

This is what makes each person stronger on the inside. Recognizing how human we are, how feeble, how weak and how much we need the strength of God to assist. There is so much truth, humility and depth found in each page of the Word of God. You can come to feel as if you are writing the words too. He is with us and strengthening us by that word day by day. Just like you see that cat hanging on the limb by one arm. Gravity is pulling him down. All his struggles and strength leaving him. But what we don't see is the other arm holding him up. That is how God is with us. That is why we have not fallen or dropped completely! When you feel yourself slipping away, you feel like you fell, you see everything at your feet but you did not fall away at all. God is holding us up the entire time. "My righteousness draws near speedily, my salvation is on the way, and **my arm** will bring justice to the nations. The islands will look to me and wait in hope for **my arm**." Isaiah 51:5

Try every day of your life: Trust, Dwell, Feed, Delight & Commit! Trust in God for all the stages of your life. Believe that He is building you up and has already designed the path for you to walk in. Dwell in His presence because He is there with you even when you don't feel it, He is right there with you. Feed on the word of God every single day and make the time necessary to provide nourishment to your body, soul and mind. Delight yourself in Him by discovering everlasting joy with the One who provides. All that this world can offer is temporary fulfillment but God brings an everlasting fulfillment. And finally just surrender all and commit your way to the Lord. Leave God in charge of your every move and your every decision. Make Him a part of that by praying every day. He promises to guide you and lead you. Don't keep holding on to what is gone and past. Let it go and just let it be. We have to move on and move forward so that we can obtain all that God has for us. Trust that He ordained all things for you. That God knows and understands you. Even when things are difficult. After all He is the one who made you, so who can know you better than that.

To allow the building –you must let go! Letting go doesn't always happen at once. It happens with consistency! No matter how we feel, stand firm on His Word because that is sovereign. Above all else, nothing can come close to the things of God. It is certainly my own personal life lesson.

> *"For every house is built by someone, but God is the Builder of everything,"* Hebrews 3:4 (New International Version)

Just like moving, as we let go we learn that these become the most fragile moments. Fragile moments become powerful movements. You have to prepare, pack and proportion everything timely. Packing in general is fragile. It is emotional. Is such a powerful statement in itself. It says so much… Because it is such a delicate moment, there are mixed emotions, crazy busy rushing, some excitement and plenty of expectation. All these things flooding through at once… I felt in my spirit as I prepared to move work locations, "Pack just what you need, you can't take everything but take enough so that you won't drown moving forward! Sometimes there is NO FORMAL GOODBYE! You just have to go… It is all part of the **let go and let God**!"

As 2015 was quickly coming to an end, I was so thankful

because God didn't wait for the clock to strike midnight on January 1 to begin a physical change. The change He has always placed over me was a NOW change!!! Ended the year already in a new place... I told my family and friends, "Rejoice with me! I am super happy!"

God is saying,

"Don't you see it! It is happening NOW!" <3

> *Forget what happened before, And do not think about the past. Look at the new thing I am going to do. It's already happening. Don't you see it?* Isaiah 43:18-19 (New Century Version)

I am looking at the new thing! I am looking at the new places God is taking me! I am looking to Him for all things. I want to worship Him with all of my life.

People are asking me, "OH MY GOD where are you going? Are you being promoted? Is this a new role?"

I am like, "I have no idea, I am just moving!"

But for me–it is a promotion in every way! God is taking me to a new place and as appealing as offers may be elsewhere –what God is doing in my life is actually MORE appealing and worthwhile. Many won't understand. Many will frown down. But this is the will of the Lord for my life, I know it is a part of my process for **all** things new! It was a chapter that needed to be closed entirely, so the memories that had to go can be left behind in this place. I will be leaving here rejoicing, smiling, and with much expectation. Even though there will be patch roads ahead–it is a **NEW** patch and that is what makes the difference for me.

In these fragile moments of life, we don't want to mess things up. We don't want to miss a thing. We keep what is valuable and necessary. Everything else that is clutter, we chuck it! It only makes the transition easier.

Transition is the movement, passage, or change from one position, state, stage, subject, concept, etc., to another; change.

This is all part of the revolution! We become the *novaturient*! New word we learned from bible study, which is desiring or seeking POWERFUL change in one's life, behavior or situation. We are seeking this powerful change!

That is my prayer! I want to get this change right. I don't want to mess up. He is changing me. My desires have changed. I have a desire to serve Him with all of me. I have a hope to live for Him. I don't want to fall off to the left. I just want to keep this RIGHT. Once and for all. The way I started this year will NOT be how I end. I am going to smile again, laugh again, live again and love again. I can't get this wrong! I cannot!

My faith and trust is in God throughout the transition and I know that He is with me! I know! He has taken me through this year and it has been a violent change but necessary! I never thought I would be able to get through it. But I did and I still am....

God is within her, she will not fall; God will help her at break of day. Psalm 46:5 (New International Version)

This fragile moment of mine has become the most monumental milestone! God is within me…

My friend! God is within you…as you are reading this…HE IS IN YOU!!! So when everyone else doesn't understand exactly what is going on around you or through you…as long as YOU know, it is OKAY! You will be at perfect peace. You will be at liberty. You will have reached a plateau where you have become seriously immovable in Christ! Your faith, hope, trust and love in Him has become **steadfast.** Because you know you finally did it… despite all the opposition!

YOU DID IT!

YOU MADE IT!

YOU SAW HIM IN YOU, TO MAKE THAT HAPPEN!

Leaving all of this in the hands of God is the way that we take. What a beautiful and amazing *fragile moment* to live through!

REBUILT: Beginning the Ending

PIECE 27
MORE THAN A THORN

Have you ever been one to ask during your journey about those piercing things? Have you asked Him constantly, "Dear Lord, remove this from me! I can't have this anymore as a thorn in my life!" Thorns hurt! For three times the Apostle Paul asked and received his answer. Maybe you are in that same situation... Asking God repeatedly to take something away so that you can be free, the next day arrives, and still that plague is present.

> *"Even though I have received such wonderful revelations from God. So to keep me from becoming proud, I was given a thorn in my flesh, a messenger from Satan to torment me and keep me from becoming proud. Three different times I begged the Lord to take it away. Each time he said, "My grace is all you need. My power works best in weakness." Now I am glad to boast about my weaknesses, so that the power of Christ can work through me. That's why I take pleasure in my*

weaknesses, and in the insults, hardships, persecutions, and troubles that I suffer for Christ. For when I am weak, then I am strong." 2 Corinthians 12:7-10 (New Living Translation)

Clearly, there was something here tormenting Paul… Day and night. A thorn [something that wounds, annoys, or causes discomfort]. Paul had this. But he also had a deep relationship with God to carry him through. The bible provides plenty of history and information but many occasions the real detail that would probably be helpful is not disclosed.

What was it???

What was the thing that was tormenting Apostle Paul? Or better yet, what is the thing that is tormenting you?

Past mistakes.
A breakup.
A memory.
A divorce.
An ailment.
A bad job.
A lost loved one.
Abuse.
Poverty.
Something missing.
Something stolen.
A bad experience.

There are so many things that could bring us torment. Torment is to afflict with great bodily or mental suffering;

pain; to worry or annoy excessively; to throw into commotion; stir up; disturb; it is a state of great bodily or mental suffering; agony; misery. What is the thing that is causing an uproar within your soul? Something that is throwing your thoughts into commotion? What is disturbing your peace or joy? What is causing you to suffer silently or openly? What is that thing that is making you absolutely miserable day in and day out?

How can we really bypass all that mess and torment when it simply WON'T GO AWAY!!!

Accepting

Embracing

Surrendering

These are three things that will take you to that place where God's power will work BEST in your weakness.

ACCEPT

> *"Don't worry about anything; instead, pray about everything. Tell God what you need, and thank Him for all He has done. Then you will experience God's peace, which exceeds anything we can understand. His peace will guard your hearts and minds as you live in Christ Jesus. And now, dear brothers and sisters, one final thing. Fix your thoughts on what is true, and honorable, and right, and pure, and lovely, and admirable. Think about things that are excellent and worthy of praise. Keep putting into practice all you*

learned and received from me—everything you heard from me and saw me doing. Then the God of peace will be with you. How I praise the Lord that you are concerned about me again. I know you have always been concerned for me, but you didn't have the chance to help me. Not that I was ever in need, for I have learned how to be content with whatever I have. I know how to live on almost nothing or with everything. I have learned the secret of living in every situation, whether it is with a full stomach or empty, with plenty or little. For I can do everything through Christ, who gives me strength." Philippians 4:6-13 NLT

The Word tells us to accept [to take or receive (something offered); receive with approval or favor; to agree or consent to; accede to; respond or answer affirmatively to]. We receive His Word. To learn how to be content in whatever we have. To make the best of it with our attitudes. To fix our thoughts on good things when the thorn is trying to bring them into a huge commotion. We tackle all that with all the things that are good. When the enemy is bombarding our minds constantly... We have to combat with the Word of God. Now we bombard our mind with things that are good and QUICKLY! When an enemy is coming at you with a sword your first reaction should be to PROTECT and shield yourself! Or you fight back! You don't just allow the blow! Why would you purposely allow yourself to get hurt? No.... FIGHT BACK! Protect yourself! Protect your mind! Protect your space! Protect what you have left!!!

EMBRACE

> *"Wisdom is a tree of life to those who embrace her; happy are those who hold her tightly. By wisdom the LORD founded the earth; by understanding he created the heavens. By His knowledge the deep fountains of the earth burst forth, and the dew settles beneath the night sky. My child, don't lose sight of common sense and discernment. Hang on to them, for they will refresh your soul. They are like jewels on a necklace. They keep you safe on your way, and your feet will not stumble. You can go to bed without fear; you will lie down and sleep soundly. You need not be afraid of sudden disaster or the destruction that comes upon the wicked, for the LORD is your security. He will keep your foot from being caught in a trap."* Proverbs 3:18-26 NLT

There is a way to overcome sleepless nights. We need to practice wisdom day in and day out! The more that we embrace wisdom by doing correct things the more God will keep our feet from being caught in the trap of the enemy's schemes! The enemy is constant at telling you the lie… And you believe it! Just like that! But it is time for God's people to stand in truth! To stand on His Word as our guide! Stop believing the lies… Lies make you die in a solitary place! Truth makes you live in a functioning place! Conduct your own personal analysis… Where are you? Are you in a good place? Or bad place? What's keeping you there?

God is giving you all the tools you need through His Word

to survive! To come out of any dark place. Be wise... Redeeming the time for the days are evil and the enemy is working diligently to scoop you in with his demise. Don't go there!

SURRENDER

> *"So humble yourselves under the mighty power of God, and at the right time He will lift you up in honor. Give all your worries and cares to God, for He cares about you. Stay alert! Watch out for your great enemy, the devil. He prowls around like a roaring lion, looking for someone to devour. Stand firm against him, and be strong in your faith. Remember that your family of believers all over the world is going through the same kind of suffering you are. In His kindness God called you to share in His eternal glory by means of Christ Jesus. So after you have suffered a little while, He will restore, support, and strengthen you, and He will place you on a firm foundation."* 1 Peter 5:6-10 (New Living Translation)

We all suffer for a little. To some it feels like forever. What we need is to be placed on this firm foundation. We have to humble ourselves really low and surrender ALL to God. We should not just place only a few things before Him when He is asking us to give Him EVERYTHING! You can't have two sets of hands on a steering wheel to drive to your destination. It is always the one set of hands. Let it be God's and not yours. Stop trying to do everything on your own efforts for that will only take you so far in life. But when you let God have full control of your life by allowing

Him to lead you only then will you experience that power over your weakness! You have to give it to God. Stop waiting for other things to get you by when God is the one that will take you THROUGH!

So next time that thorn pops up to torment you… Shut it down with the Word of God. Accept all the good that God IS doing on your behalf even if you don't feel it. He is working. Embrace wisdom and right choices every step of your life. The Holy Spirit is your anchor and support to prompt you through the process. He is there… Don't drown out His voice with yours. And finally, surrender ALL to God… Even this thorn. When you think it is too much, tell Him again. He NEVER EVER gets tired of hearing you talk to Him. The more you do, the more all else will fade. His power and presence will be with you ALWAYS…. More than any thorn could ever be.

You can boast in that thorn or weakness. For God is giving all the strength you need to pull through victoriously. You're still here … right! So make the best of it.

REBUILT: Beginning the Ending

PIECE 28
BLACK BUTTERFLIES

Days, weeks, months and moments were passing us by. Progress was evident. We were trying a lot of personal time and new family time. It was different. Many nice moments God was giving us. For December, we went to see The Rockettes in the city! We passed this fixture on our way to go to the show and I had to stop and take a picture. I love pictures.

From the distance, I saw the shape of the butterfly but it was dark. As I got closer, I saw how intriguing this display really was. As dark as it was…they were butterflies intertwined, with all their wings stretched out. Worthy of capturing.

Wikipedia states that black is the darkest color, the result of the absence of or complete absorption of light. It is the opposite of white (the combined spectrum of color or light). It is an achromatic color, literally a color without color or hue. It is one of the four primary colors in the CMYK color model, along with cyan, yellow, and magenta, used in color printing to produce all the other colors. [WOW]

Black was one of the first colors used by artists in Neolithic cave paintings. In the 14th century, it began to be worn by royalty, the clergy, judges and government officials in much of Europe. It became the color worn by English romantic poets, businessmen and statesmen in the 19th century, and a high fashion color in the 20th century.

Now black makes a statement!

It is the absence of light, yet we know that it must exist in order for light to be present [Isaiah 60]!

> **God is the Lord, and He has given us light; bind the sacrifice with cords to the horns of the altar.** Psalm 118:27 (New King James Version)

> **The Lord is God, and He has made His light shine on us. With boughs in hand, join in the festal procession up to the horns of the altar.** Psalm 118:27 (New International Version)

We are people made of dust. Off the ground. In a dark place, we had come to the light. God breathed into the man and gave us life. Darkness had to be present. Then light overpowered.

Sometimes we go through the darkest places in life but we never lose our shape. We become those black butterflies that are so intertwined. They are all very beautiful…even though they are black. Color becomes irrelevant. Past is removed. Concept is discovered. Depth is understood. For why is everything so contrary? Why such a fight against the light? Two fights… the dark against the light. At all times, that is present.

> ***I shall not die, but live, and declare the works of the Lord. The Lord has chastened me severely, but has not given me over to death.*** Psalm 118:17-18 (New King James Version)

The enemy is chasing us down in such a way. The struggle is present. For the battle is written out in the Word for us to take heed and exceed! We can win the war. The Lord is our support and consistently showing us the way because THERE IS A WAY!!

The writer continues to express his constant battle. There is written a way…

> ***All nations surrounded me, But in the name of the Lord, I will destroy them. They surrounded me, Yes, they surrounded me; But in the name of the Lord, I will destroy them. They surrounded me like bees; They were quenched like a fire of thorns; For in the name of the***

> *Lord I will destroy them. You pushed me violently, that I might fall, But the Lord helped me. The Lord is my strength and song, And He has become my salvation.*
> Psalm 118:10-14 (New King James Version)

He wrote in the name of the Lord I WOULD destroy them. He could declare that. With God on his side, he had the ability, authority, strength and power to resist and destroy his enemies!!!

He was that man... that lived in the supernatural and came to the natural. He had tremendous victories on Sunday and then had to go to work on Monday. He had to fight off his enemies and push past his weekly challenges. He wanted to conquer his Monday! He wanted the victory every day of his life... not just at a worship service! HIS BATTLES WERE SCARY AND INTENSE! It seemed never-ending and unyielding. He waged war! In EVERY aspect.

Now he didn't speak of a dark place but a forgotten place. A place that seemed hidden from all the rest. This part was not on display and not public. Beyond the lights, smiles, serving, singing or preaching. The prophecy is deep. The high calling is the utmost. But simultaneously with that is the Monday- it is everything contrary to that spoken word. It opposes the word, challenges and comes against that promise.

This walk has nothing to do with feelings BUT THEY ARE PRESENT! Emotions are alive. A way of escape is sought. For our mind can quickly conjure up accessible ways to react but that is not correct, it is corrupt! Why is the worthless so worthwhile? Why is the meaningless so meaningful? Why is the insignificant so significant? The futile so fruitful? The cheap so costly? The empty so full? The ineffective so effective? WHY?

Darkness had to be present. In that definition above, the darkest color was used to produce the REST! It was used for the others to be seen. It became the predominant color. It became prestigious. It became the color worn to make a statement for high governing officials. It became a color worn for great significance and to display authority! This dark color is worn in the light. The darkness was only present so that you can see the truth. This testimony is amazing! It is saying that no matter how dark it got…it was still beautiful. I didn't die from it…but I lived!

God kept me alive.

God's purpose SHALL BE FULFILLED.

All the black butterflies will be so bold and beautiful. They won't be forgotten. They will be seen. They will matter. They will shine. They will radiate. They will be so powerful in every way!

> *Teach me, O Lord, the way of Your statutes, and I shall keep it to the end. Give me understanding, and I shall keep Your law; Indeed, I shall observe it with my whole heart. Make me walk in the path of Your commandments, for I delight in it. Incline my heart to Your testimonies, and not to covetousness. Turn away my eyes from looking at worthless things, and revive me*

in Your way. Establish Your word to Your servant, who is devoted to fearing You. Turn away my reproach which I dread, for Your judgments are good. Behold, I long for Your precepts; Revive me in Your righteousness. Let Your mercies come also to me, O Lord—Your salvation according to Your word. So shall I have an answer for him who reproaches me, for I trust in Your word. And take not the word of truth utterly out of my mouth, for I have hoped in Your ordinances. So shall I keep Your law continually, forever and ever. And I will walk at liberty, for I seek Your precepts. I will speak of Your testimonies also before kings, and will not be ashamed. And I will delight myself in Your commandments, which I love. My hands also I will lift up to Your commandments, which I love, And I will meditate on Your statutes. Remember the word to Your servant, Upon which You have caused me to hope. This is my comfort in my affliction, For Your word has given me life. Psalm 119:33-50 (New King James Version)

Writings from black butterflies... who trusted in this word.

"Your word is a lamp to my feet and a light to my path."
Psalm 119:105 (New King James Version)

When I consider where I was a year ago from today, my entire soul does rejoice! It is not merely that I have proven to man but that I have connected with God so that He would lead me in the way that is everlasting–and that I would ACCEPT!

A year ago, I was selfish. A year ago, I only thought about

my ways. A year ago, I wanted to pursue everything that I thought was best for me despite what God ordained for me. A year ago, I was heavily deceived and confused with my own calling of God and what He wanted for me as a woman. A year ago, I was bound and now I am free.

Now I know. The only path I needed to take was the one of righteousness and He would lead me to it. I desperately needed to recognize and accept just that.

Now my whole world has changed and I will follow after God all of my days. My soul does rejoice indeed!

> ***"I delight greatly in the LORD; my soul rejoices in my God. For He has clothed me with garments of salvation and arrayed me in a robe of His righteousness, as a bridegroom adorns his head like a priest, and as a bride adorns herself with her jewels."*** Isaiah 61:10 (New International Version)

God has adorned [to decorate or add beauty to] me now. Just like a bride is adorned with jewelry on her special day. Every day I am adorned with His love, His grace and His mercy! He took His righteousness and gave it to me too! Yes, my soul does rejoice because of this!

> ***"Then my soul will rejoice in the LORD and delight in His salvation."*** Psalm 35:9 (New International Version)

God is leading me down a road to goodness and wholeness. I am excited to see what He has in store for me and for His people. I keep going. I keep following. I keep doing. I keep seeking. I keep praying. I keep reading. I keep writing. I keep sharing. I keep giving and I keep believing.

For before, I abandoned all for self and now I abandon all for Him. A new focus He has shown me and this I will strive for.

- Faith
- Family
- Fellowship

This is a path of *faith*.

> *"Make me walk in the path of Your commandments, For I delight in it."* ~Psalm 119:35

> *"You comprehend my path and my lying down, and are acquainted with all my ways."* ~Psalm 139:3

> *"My child, don't go along with them! Stay far away from their paths."* ~Proverbs 1:15

> *"This Good News tells us how God makes us right in His sight. This is accomplished from start to finish by faith. As the Scriptures say, 'It is through faith that a righteous person has life.'"* ~Romans 1:17

This is a path of *family*.

> *"So now you Gentiles are no longer strangers and foreigners. You are citizens along with all of God's holy people. You are members of God's family."* ~Ephesians 2:19

> *"Therefore, whenever we have the opportunity, we should do good to everyone—especially to those in the family of faith."* ~Galatians 6:10

> *"And further, submit to one another out of reverence for Christ."* ~Ephesians 5:21

This is a path of **fellowship**.

> *"imploring us with much urgency that we would receive the gift and the fellowship of the ministering to the saints."* ~2 Corinthians 8:4

> *"not forsaking the assembling of ourselves together, as is the manner of some, but exhorting one another, and so much the more as you see the Day approaching."* ~Hebrews 10:25

> *"that their hearts may be encouraged, being knit together in love, and attaining to all riches of the full assurance of understanding, to the knowledge of the mystery of God, both of the Father and of Christ,"* ~Colossians 2:2

In light of this path, I have learned the importance to keep my faith firm in God. To have my family as a priority. And to understand the importance of fellowship for my continual growth. God will guide me in all that I do moving forward and will guide you too when you surrender a contrite heart over to Him. The road may seem rough at times but determine to follow the light that will carry you through even the darkest places. That light will never go out.

He is the light to my path.

He is the light to your path.

He is the light of the WORLD.

Now God can take this opportunity to move us in every place. The time of rebuilding is a delicate part of our life. Everything is critical. Everything is crucial. Everything has to be assembled correctly in this time.

PIECE 29

THE VICTOR

"Join with me in suffering, like a good soldier of Christ Jesus. No one serving as a soldier gets entangled in civilian affairs, but rather tries to please his commanding officer. Similarly, anyone who competes as an athlete does not receive the victor's crown except by competing according to the rules." 2 Timothy 2:3-5 (New International Version)

Around Veteran's Day, I was sitting in an honoree service, and left so influenced by the words exchanged regarding these men. They stand as soldiers that have sacrificed, served and surrendered their life to fight and protect this country. This is worthy of giving honor. These are true victors. They have survived much and can sit in a place as a representative that was put through many battles in life. They won. They fought through. They lift their hands for the victory!

Sometimes we become so mad at ourselves for being the victim.

Questioning, "WHY did I do it, WHY GOD? If I knew this would lead me wrong then why did I do it? Why?"

I kept contemplating. The focus is now more on being the victim and not the victor. This is why it is so critical to go to the Word of God for direction. What does it say? How does it advise us in these times. We don't have to be a victim. Find the truth!

The enemy doesn't love you …he lures you. His plan is to destroy you and come against your purpose. He is seeking whom he MAY devour and that does not have to be you! Be watchful! Be wise! Be warned! Because all he wants to do is bring you down with him when God has a plan for you to live for eternity with Him!

Don't allow the enemy to tap into your own personal realm! Don't allow those boundaries to be crossed! You decide! You set the pace for your progress and protection against his EVIL plans!

Nothing good comes out of what he has to offer you!!! Nothing good, so stand SHARP! Gear up and send that devil right where he belongs! If you don't even know WHY you fell prey! I am here to remind you today that there is a way! A way to win and a way out of his mess!

Humble yourselves, therefore under God's mighty hand, that He may lift you up in due time. Cast ALL your anxiety [and care] on him because He cares for

The Victor

*you. Be **ALERT** and of sober mind. Your enemy the devil prowls around like a roaring lion looking for someone to devour. **RESIST** him, standing firm in the faith, because you know that the family of believers throughout the world is undergoing the **SAME** kind of suffering.* 1 Peter 5:6-9 (New King James Version)

You are not the only one. You are not alone. The enemy LIES to you! He deceives you! He is not thinking of you like the way GOD is mindful of you. The only thing the enemy is thinking about is destroying WHO YOU ARE... Attacking your identity! Accusing your life! Opposing your future! But you MUST be reminded! Don't think on the lies! Don't buy into his corrupt nature! It won't work!!!! He is LYING! That is all he does, he is as good at it as the father of lies.

Resist the devil and he will flee from you!

That is why sometimes the enemy won't take you seriously. It is like working in the gym, selling or promoting health products and your obese. Does it work or not?!? This is truth for us. It is being extremely real with the situation. Because yes, the enemy will appear over time and look more dazzling than ever but you DO HAVE the power to resist! Now your enemy will really know!

I do not have to be a victim.... I'm a victor!

I AM more than a conqueror because I AM lives in me!

So begin telling yourself that every single time the enemy tries to attack or accuse you... I don't have a problem, I have a PROMISE! And I will remain faithful to my God!

Just as these scriptures speak on suffering for the soldier– know that we all have to experience this. It is only to make us stronger. Submit to God. Give this over to Him. He wants you to be the victor! We shall overcome and wear that victor's crown! Now instead of contemplating loss, contemplate the cost! You can do it. You can win. You are God's soldier and His grace is upon you to finish the fight. Keep reminding yourself about that crown.

But He gives us more grace.

That is why the Scripture says:

> ***"God opposes the proud but shows favor to the humble." Submit yourselves, then to God. Resist the devil and he will flee from you.*** James 4:6-7 (New International Version)

> ***I have fought the good fight, I have finished the race, I have kept the faith. Now there is in store for me the crown of righteousness, which the Lord, the righteous Judge, will award to me on that day– and not only to me, but also to all who have longed for His appearing.*** 2 Timothy 4:7-8 (New International Version)

> ***I press on toward the goal to win the prize for which God has called me heavenward in Christ Jesus.*** Philippians 3:14 (New International Version)

YOU ARE A VICTOR!!!

In all areas, we are pressing for this revolution! That we not only are that participant of a revolution but that we *become* the revolutionists! Just like Caleb—he was DIFFERENT! He came in agreement with GOD for that promised land! He was another example of a key pioneer!

> **"But because my servant Caleb has a *different* spirit and follows me wholeheartedly, I will bring him into the land he went to, and his descendants will inherit it."**
> Numbers 14:24 (New International Version)

This is the time that we shall be striving for revolutionary relationships! For our marriages, churches, homes and those that we define as the real friend that sticks closer than a brother. We will move from the friendship to sisterhood and brotherhood. That we excel to find those IN Christ as we seek to grow. It is not to leave anyone out but that we know who we latch on to that will *propel* us further into our destiny and not derail us from it! There have been way too many parasites coming forth that have hindered us all throughout the years and that has to cease. We are here to **help** each other out not drown each other… We want to seek to better ourselves and others and that must happen with a *revolutionary* mindset. That must happen with a kingdom mindset. That must happen with change.

For way too long the world has encouraged seeking after "numero uno"—SELF and what that actually does is destroy self and anyone else that even tries to come close. Now it is learning how to improve self so that when we get around to others it is going to be in a way that is *beneficial*. That is a whole new way of thinking. It is literally dissecting the book of Proverbs as it translates to handling our key relationships. Our relationship with the King, our children, our parents, our spouses, our brothers, sisters and also the friendships that need to be cultivated in the right way. There in those holy pages, it speaks to the dealings of all of that and to demonstrate improvements that will lead to flourishing, enriching and wholesome connections for life.

Many times, we have failed in this area but the good news is that we learn every time we fall how we can do it better! There is a world of opportunity ahead of us. And when we take that opportunity and couple it with the scripture and prayer—the end result will be 100% fruitfulness! The past will tell us not to try. The pain will tell us to protect. The memory will tell us to quit but the bible will tell us to renew, restore and REBUILD right relationships starting with us!

This is the one time in life where you will see the difference in doing something for you that will benefit the rest. When you have to do something for you that will be impacting. You have to make a choice to do it. No one else is going to take you there, get you there or push you there but YOU. You are going to have to decide. You are going to have to motivate you. You are going to have to preach to you. You are going to have to pray for you. You are going to have to fast for you. If you want to see it, then you are going to have to do it. The waiting is only crushing you. The complacency is only delaying you.

We have to go-go-go!

The Victor

Acceleration is before us!

What are you going to do about it?

Where will you be?

Who will you be with?

What will you do?

How will you do it?

If God gave you a map, now you have to look at it, read it, study it, declare it, walk it out and live it out. Stop waiting for another invitation. Accelerate yourself, make the decision that this is YOUR TIME to go and grow! And who will stand beside you will be evidence of those primary decisions.

Many of us are still hanging on the balance beam. Destiny is at hand and the "I don't know" is on the mind. We are swaying back and forth of the "I don't know" for way too long. You can't have someone else give you your destiny. It is not going to be handed to you. But it will have to be YOU to take hold of that destiny. It will never take root or be deposited firmly until YOU TAKE IT FOR YOU! That is the moment that becomes the maker! Everything else is just a balance. Here is where you will see who you really are and what you are made of. You have a huge work to do!

Take it! Try Him! And watch how everything falls right into place.

To walk away is just a delay for you and you will see how

nothing goes anywhere but only cause further confusion. It is time for you to set the bar, for you to raise the standards and for you to run with it!

MAKE IT HAPPEN!

Stop living in the past! Stop doubting yourself! Stop letting all these things hinder your progress. The only one leaving you stuck is you… especially when you see things happening for others! There is something that can happen for you too! You keep wanting for the SAME THING that everybody else has when God is trying to give you something unique that is fit for you!

God did not forget about you! He did not leave you out. We are the ones that actually leave ourselves out every single time we stay stagnant and moping along the way! We have to become more aggressive at taking hold of our **peace** and our **promise**! You must refuse to be refused, deny to be denied and move yourself forward at all costs! Of course, it is not going to be easy –you are going to bleed right through it. You are going to scream and cry but AS YOU ARE IN IT, you are going to see that you are living in the purpose of God. You are **pulling through the purpose**!!!

For HUGE destiny, there will be HUGE opposition!

It has nothing to do with us but everything to do with God's plan! This becomes a place –a moment—a stepping-stone for you. This becomes the preparation, the rehabilitation and the deliverance so that you can reach the place where God sets off the activation for your ministry! You will be pushed, thrown, stretched and pressed as you continue

The Victor

down the route that leads RIGHT!

Many will be a part of the revolution in the last days but not everyone is a revolutionist! Not everyone is a pioneer—a world changer. It is those that are not just going to partake or participate but that will **propel** themselves into PURPOSE!

They will launch out!

They will make it happen!

They will be so uncomfortable with being comfortable. They will be the one that must do SOMETHING!

The one that can't sit still.

The one that can't keep watching.

The one that can't keep waiting.

The WATER WALKER!

The doer!

The thinker!

The visionary!

The eagle!

Take yourself beyond the mental loop of madness! Stop living in your own personal 40-year long wilderness and WALK TO THAT PROMISED LAND! And the ones that are going to possess that land with you will WALK IT OUT TOO!

Those are the revolutionists! That have decided that doing the same thing over and over again is insanity that they **REFUSE** to tolerate that!

As the years continue—it will be a completely new view! We need that sharp vision to approach 2020!

Keep taking those ardent steps to your victory!

PIECE 30

PULLING THROUGH THE PROMISE

Against all hope, Abraham in hope believed and so became the father of many nations, just as it had been said to him, "So shall your offspring be." Without weakening in his faith, he faced the fact that his body was as good as dead—since he was about a hundred years old—and that Sarah's womb was also dead. Yet he did not waver through unbelief regarding the promise of God, but was strengthened in his faith and gave glory to God, being fully persuaded that God had power to do what He had promised. This is why "it was credited to him as righteousness." Romans 4:18-22 (New International Version)

I remember some time about 3 years prior that we were about to be senior pastors of our church and we had no idea what we were going to do with our current situation. We were going through another serious rough patch. My husband and I decided to have lunch on New Year's Eve, before we went into the new year and he said these words to me that propelled us into our destiny. I will never forget them…

"I am not sure about this situation, I am not sure about us, I am not sure about work…anything! But one thing that I am sure of and it is that God called me to pastor Mission United International church. So if you are going to be on board with that or not…I am."

Six months later, we became the senior pastors of MUI Church, Yonkers. Did that stop our trials and tribulations? Did that make our issues and trying times disappear? NO– it did not. In fact, can I share this–things got *worse* before they got better!

We were against all hope! Yet did not waver at the promise!

In making any difficult decision, we will typically encounter **MORE** opposition. The reason that we encounter such opposition is so that we become stronger. You don't grow strong over weak circumstances and happy bliss fairy tales. You grow stronger by **overcoming** trials! We are not just made to conquer but we are made to be MORE than conquerors. Meaning that we will be known for the battles we have won and not just *one* but many!

I was reading in the book, "Four Doors" by Richard Paul Evans where he wrote the following profound statement as it relates to **adversity**.

Pulling Through The Promise

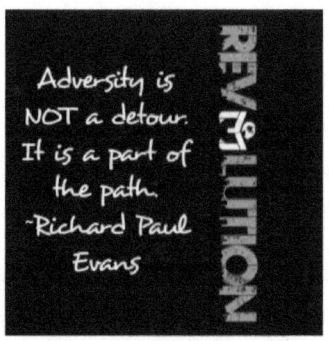

Adversity is NOT a detour. It is a part of the path.
–Richard Paul Evans

That seemed to be the case always for me. The adversity that I have faced never bypassed me. It actually came most times to try to overtake me. Issues seemed unbearable and overwhelming. But even through all that, I had a keen vision to see an ocean of possibilities that God would do what He said that He would do. Not what I could do…because our human strength is so flawed BUT through God—we do valiantly! Through God, we do triumphantly. Through God, we are able. He is the MAIN DOOR that I will always dare and choose to walk through.

It is always going to be some sort of a fight. We can do it. But we have to be so dependent upon God as we do things. He is with us and in us. Yes, He is fighting for us but we will see the effort that we have to put in using the Word as our weapon for warfare! There will always be a fight and that is when we will experience the victory.

> *For though we live in the world, we do not wage war as the world does. The weapons we fight with are not the weapons of the world. On the contrary, they have divine power to demolish strongholds. We demolish arguments and every pretension that sets itself up against the*

> *knowledge of God, and we take captive every thought to make it obedient to Christ. And we will be ready to punish every act of disobedience, once your obedience is complete.* 2 Corinthians 10:3-6 (New International Version)

We have the power to demolish everything that comes against the Word of God and against the promises that He has given us. We need to confess and believe that the same way that Abraham did. We have weapons in order to combat the adversity that so strongly presses upon that promise.

Be reminded that when the enemy comes at you to challenge your destiny and purpose that you have the strongest weapons ever that WORK! When situations look as good as dead… When things look impossible… When you feel like you have come *against all hope*–use the (S)WORD and cut it down.

God-will-do-what-He-promised!

> *Finally, my brethren, be strong in the Lord and in the power of His might. Put on the whole armor of God, that you may be able to stand against the wiles of the devil. For we do not wrestle against flesh and blood, but against principalities, against powers, against the rulers of the darkness of this age, against spiritual hosts of wickedness in the heavenly places. Therefore, take up the whole armor of God, that you may be able to withstand in the evil day, and having done all, to stand. Stand therefore, having girded your waist with truth,*

having put on the breastplate of righteousness, and having shod your feet with the preparation of the gospel of peace; above all, taking the shield of faith with which you will be able to quench all the fiery darts of the wicked one. And take the helmet of salvation, and the sword of the Spirit, which is the word of God; praying always with all prayer and supplication in the Spirit, being watchful to this end with all perseverance and supplication for all the saints— and for me, that utterance may be given to me, that I may open my mouth boldly to make known the mystery of the gospel, for which I am an ambassador in chains; that in it I may speak boldly, as I ought to speak. Ephesians 6:10-20 (New King James Version)

These are the last days! And times are going to get MORE intense! Just as we are sailing past the hustle and bustle, we will get through all of these.

My heart does have a deep concern for those unable to turn

from such torment. I can only ease myself and my peace of mind by keeping them in prayer.

As for me, my family and the church… God is keeping us through every season. I hear Him loud in my soul these days saying…

Can you bear it?

Yes, I can, God! With YOU, I can do all these things. At church on Sunday, the last Sunday service of 2015, I stood with a huge smile on my face. I could not contain it! Hopefully contagious because God has just been so good to me! I can bear it! What started out as the year from hell and back turned out to be the year of healing and triumph!

I was so ashamed, upset, downcast and LITERALLY DESTROYED! I didn't even want to walk in the doors of church anymore. Tears became my food day and night as the psalmist declared! But THANKS BE TO MY GOD WHO HAS DELIVERED ME FROM EVERY TRIAL! I am no longer in shame, ruins or brokenness for He took all that and placed His redemptive covering over me! He has crowned me with glory! With loving-kindness and tender mercies!!! What looked like the worst year turned out to be the BEST! Sitting in January and now standing as we push to another January! And preaching God's victory!

I love HIM! And I will shout it from the rooftops for my God has saved me and pulled me out of the PIT OF DEATH! Now I will do, go, say, walk and enter into all the places that HE has for me!

So thankful!

And so the apostle declares…

> *"But know this, that in the last days, perilous times will come: For men will be lovers of themselves, lovers of money, boasters, proud, blasphemers, disobedient to parents, unthankful, unholy, unloving, unforgiving, slanderers, without self-control, brutal, despisers of good, traitors, headstrong, haughty, lovers of pleasure rather than lovers of God, having a form of godliness but denying its power. And from such people turn away! For of this sort are those who creep into households and make captives of gullible women loaded down with sins, led away by various lusts, always learning and never able to come to the knowledge of the truth. Now as Jannes and Jambres resisted Moses, so do these also resist the truth: men of corrupt minds, disapproved concerning the faith; but they will progress no further, for their folly will be manifest to all, as theirs also was. But you have carefully followed my doctrine, manner of life, purpose, faith, longsuffering, love, perseverance, persecutions, afflictions, which happened to me at Antioch, at Iconium, at Lystra—what persecutions I endured. And out of them all the Lord delivered me."* II Timothy 3:1-11 (New King James Version)

Out of EVERY–SINGLE–TRIAL and tribulation the Lord HAS delivered me! Out of them ALL!!! He didn't leave me for dead like Glass in the movie "The Revenant!"

I shared the BEAR scene with the congregation! So sorry to have spoiled it for folks that did not get to see this gruesome but riveting film starring Leonardo DiCaprio and Tom Hardy.

It was a lengthy brutal scene about 15 minutes into the movie that took a turn leading to the primary theme. The character Glass survives a horrible bear attack leaving him left for dead. The scene showed everything! This man being ripped apart by a huge angry bear! He was thrown, torn and shredded by the sharpest nails! I could barely watch but I had to see this FIGHT! Man and Beast!!! The man barely able to move managed to get a shot in after having the riffle flung away at first attack! After missing the takedown of the bear, he finds a pocketknife and begins hacking away at the bear during MORE furious bites and tears!!!

The bear was using this poor man as a toy! Same way the enemy is trying to toy with us! BUT IF WE FIGHT!!!

If we resist!
If we persist!
If we pull out ALL our weapons!

We surely can bear it and take out the "grizzly bear" from our way! We just NEED to fight with what God has given us!

USE THAT (S)WORD!!!

So that you are ABLE to bear the BEARS in your life and slay every single one!!!

<u>To bear</u> is to hold up; support; to hold or remain firm under (a load); to bring forth (young); give birth to; to produce by natural growth; to hold up under; be capable of; to press or push against; to hold or carry (oneself, one's body, one's head, etc.); to conduct (oneself); to suffer; endure; undergo; to sustain without yielding or suffering injury and to tolerate.

In a film like this, it creates an image for us. Even if it appears unrealistic. This was a just prime example of how one is BEARING the bear!!! A conqueror indeed with a new purpose driven inside to him to SURVIVE!

I am not sure of your "grizzly" type of situation but rest assured just like the three Hebrew boys in Daniel 3 endured the flames seven times stronger… So can we! The people absent of God were not able to survive the flames bringing the boys near the fire! They died just going NEAR!!! But look how powerful our God is that being IN IT IS SAFER! It will never, never… EVER take you out!

In the darkest and roughest places in life come forth the most beautiful and brightest things!!! That is how you look pulling through the fire, the storms and all the grizzlies in your life! It is amazing to see how God is using you to pull right through.

We are still standing this year and not only alive but thriving! God did that! <3

REBUILT: Beginning the Ending

Can we bear it?
YES! We can!
Yes, we can pull through!
We are rebuilt!

Appendix

What you will find is a revolutionary heart at the end of your process.

God gave me a new heart – a revolutionary and rebuilt heart.

As God continues to move in a mighty way, we can begin experiencing that spiritual tsunami! He starts to overwhelm us with glorious moments! It is absolutely beautiful. Especially when we have been down those rough roads.

The other side to that is the enemy is also coming fiercely to fight us tooth and nail. Since the enemy has been cast on this earth—and as long as we live here TOO, then we are just going to have to duke it out! Issues start to surface; he tries to snatch away that word and then comes the contention…BUT WE WILL CONQUER!!!

"Contention is just an indicator that CHANGE is necessary." Ron Carpenter, Jr.

Where do we begin? With a revolution of the *heart*! God is processing us and we will see it and live it.

For the change to begin, it is by the power of character that we will see the results. That is hard work! How much are will willing to change… to go to God and say… HERE IS MY HEART! Take it, mold it and **change** it!

A revolution is a sudden, complete or marked change in something, it is a turn or thorough replacement. Sometimes we can't change or grow in a thing because there is just too much clutter there. Something is vacating the place exactly where God needs to fill.

**When you start to remove the clutter,
You begin to make room for the BEST things!**

> *I will give you a new heart and put a new spirit within you; I will take the heart of stone out of your flesh and give you a heart of flesh. I will put My Spirit within you and cause you to walk in My statutes, And you will keep My judgments and do them.* Ezekiel 36:26-28 (New King James Version)

Before God gives you something new, He has to get rid of the old. Everything else that is taking the place of God. Remember that God is going to destroy what destroys you!

He will remove, abolish, amputate, cut out/off, detach, **dethrone**, erase, pull out, purge and **SEPARATE**.

Why do we keep carrying and nurturing things that HURT us? Why do we keep things that don't belong to us or from God? Just GET RID OF IT!

Your first place of growth is to remove all the things that hinder us, even if it is a mindset. Throw away trinkets, letters, clothing, key chains…if the memory ties you to pain then TRASH it!

He shall remove all the fat and burn it on the altar. Leviticus 4:19 (New International Version)

The altar is symbolic of the presence of God. It is a holy place. We can't grow or function if we don't remove the "fat" from our lives. And it is obvious–we know that it is not good for us.

I will gather you from the countries where you have been scattered, and I will give you back the land of Israel again. They will return to it and remove all its vile images and detestable idols-I will give them an undivided heart and put a new spirit in them. Ezekiel 11:17-19 (New International Version)

We can't have that 1 foot in and 1 foot out. That is halfheartedly and half committed living. The Psalmist wrote in 119:2, "seek Him with the WHOLE heart!"

RENEW

What do we need to renew? Our ways and our mind! This is to <u>reestablish</u>, to make effective, begin or take up again. This says–Let's try this again the RIGHT way. Your walk, life, love, relationships, work life or ministry. How–all things new. If God is doing a new thing in you then why do you keep doing the old things still? It is called HABIT! We are creatures of habit.

> *Forget what happened before, And do not think about the past. Look at the new thing I am going to do. It's already happening. Don't you see it?* Isaiah 43:18-19 (New Century Version)

Break the cycle! If mommy and daddy did it–doesn't mean you have to do it. If it happened to all your aunts and uncles, that doesn't have to be you. We cannot progress as long as we keep holding on to past practices. If it happened in relationship A that does not mean it will happen in relationship B.

TRY AGAIN!

We give the enemy and others WAY too much room and permission when God is calling US to raise the standards.

We are people that are more than capable of change. Change your thinking and it will change your actions. How? The WORD! You can't keep having a mentality that says, "Oh but I am like this! This is me!" The evidence of change is CHANGE and that my friend is very much possible when you give your whole heart to God. He turns it!

> *The king's heart is in the hand of the Lord, like the rivers of water; He turns it wherever He wishes.* Proverbs 21:1 (New King James Version)

Time to RENEW the mind... the Apostle Paul wrote, "I urge you by the tender mercies of God...." in Romans 12:1-2. We **must** renew our minds. Surrender all. History does not have to repeat itself in your home. That transformation of the mind needs to take place!

RESTORE

We need to bring back into existence. If it was broke – **it can be fixed!** Being broken doesn't mean that it doesn't work. It just means that it is not functioning *PROPERLY*! Make it right **now**. God promises with this new heart to restore the years. Stop thinking "its lost time, lost years or lost love." Make it different. Make it right, WITH God. David was broken and wrote in Psalm 51:12, "Restore to me the joy of your salvation."

Remember the latter will always be greater! God does save the best for last. Stop thinking... "I'm last, I'm late, I'm old or I still don't have it." God saves the **BEST** for last!

> *So I will restore to you the years... that the swarming locust has eaten, the crawling locusts, the consuming locusts, and the chewing locusts...* Joel 2:25 (New King James Version)

Any of you still have some stuff swarming over you.

God has this!

REBUILD

This is where true work takes place with the strongest roots and foundation ever! If you ever felt like you survived, and there is so much rubble to work through… this is the building! There is no going back when you rebuild, it is because the old stuff is gone and YES, it is hard. Now you're alive to thrive!

In Nehemiah 1 & 2 they fixed together! Many times, we fail at things because it was a joint effort. Now rebuilt – the better way. It is a team effort. Nehemiah said, "Let's rebuild!" They responded, "Yes, let's rebuild!" And they did it!

Now rebuild – the better way, God's way, through His word, His grace, His redemption and by His plans! Don't stay in a mindset, "But it is a mess now." If it is ruined –good! RUIN us Lord! So that we can reflect You!

Let it be rebuilt," and of the temple, "Let its foundations be laid."' Isaiah 44:28 (New International Version)

Allow God to do that work **in** you, **for** you and **through** you. So that those finger-pointing experts can say, "WOW…. God did that! That dysfunctional family became the deliverance family!"

Chains are broken!

We are in that quick marked change!

The enemy is mad. The trials are real yes, but we get to see a REAL God break through our night and turn our mourning into dancing. He takes the tears to water the roots…deep roots, so that we are so grounded in Him. Our family found hope and purpose filled in this scripture…

Appendix

They will rebuild the ancient ruins and restore the places long devastated; they will renew the ruined cities that have been devastated for generations. Isaiah 61:4 (New International Version)

Let's start that REAL revolution. It begins with the heart that will impact the rest! So that we will see the revolution in our own personal life, home, job, church and everywhere else that our feet tread upon!

The journey to an approved you is already in the works. There is no stopping now but progressing. There will be growth, some good days and bad but we are able if we consistently feed ourselves with all the tools we need to create that relationship with God and a healthy atmosphere that will edify us moving forward.

I have learned a lot in the past year. I learned that my life belongs completely to God. I have learned the family is a serious priority that requires quality care. I learned that my inner joy was going to always be present as I maintain not just a relationship with God but an intimate one! I learned that marriage is not supposed to be the governing source that makes you *happy*—it makes you *holy* as God covers that union. It is strategic. It is sacred. It is a sacrifice. I learned that my children are my number one supporters for us. I learned that the church—is really comprised of a body of Christ that seeks the Lord no matter what! They stick together to fulfill the purpose of Christ. Lastly, that no matter *how bad* things get, it is never beyond repair—God CAN renew, restore and rebuild!

I hope and I pray that all the words put together have edified and encouraged you along the way. Keep some of these words handy and keep them in your heart especially those that are scripture based. I try every day with my entire mind to continue in the things that God has for me. I keep focused. I keep trying to better myself at the time that I help to better others. There is no other way but through God and through an authentic relationship with the ONLY ONE that will take you through the journey. Your entire life is a journey and God will take you through the doors. Just keep yourself prepared and ready to embark on the territory that He has stationed just for you. Trust and know God intimately every day. He will never steer you in the wrong way. Don't quit, don't give up and don't think the worst when the rough days come. God is your source for a rebuilt life. He is your source for a new and improved you.

> *At least there is hope for a tree: If it is cut down, it will sprout again, And its new shoots will NOT fail!* Job 14:7

~ Christina Cruz-Mendez

About Me

Christina Cruz-Mendez was born and raised in New York City. and currently resides in Westchester County. She is as a lead pastor at Mission United International Church in Yonkers, NY working alongside her husband Juan A. Mendez Jr., Senior Pastor. They have been together for 24 years with two beautiful children that God has blessed them with, Cassandra and Samuel. This makes us the family of four – "JusChrist4". She is a professional worker in area of Communications and Human Resources. She has been a Christian and active in ministry for about 15 years. Through all the rocky and smooth roads in life, she is beyond humbled that God has brought her this far in life to share with the world what He is doing in her, through her and for her. She has a passion to read and write. It is her outlet from all. Through this she is able to find inspiration and share it with the world. It is very deep, it is intimate, but it is also necessary for the time that we live in. Truth is our shield and buckler. In order for us to be a tower of safety in reaching the lives of others, we need to be real about our struggles and successes. God is fighting for us. We have the victory always.

Blog Page and Websites:

www.juschrist4.com
www.muiwomen.com
www.muichurch.org

www.ingramcontent.com/pod-product-compliance
Lightning Source LLC
Chambersburg PA
CBHW030851170426
43193CB00009BA/566